The
HUMANISTIC
SOCIAL WORK
Project

:

Humane & Spiritual Qualities of the Professional in Humanistic
Social Work: *Humanistic Social Work – The THIRD WAY in Theory
and Practice*

Edition Entirely in English

Author:
Petru Stefaroi

Cover:
Ionut Platon, Petru Stefaroi

ISBN-13: 978-1508827719
ISBN-10: 1508827710

CreateSpace, Charleston SC, an Amazon.com Company
4900 LaCross Road, North Charleston, SC 29406, USA

Include References and Bibliography (Works Consulted)

Paperback: 224 pages
Product Dimensions: 9 x 6 inches / 15.24 x 22.86 cm

*Petru Stefaroi*

# HUMANE & SPIRITUAL
## QUALITIES
## OF THE PROFESSIONAL
## IN
# HUMANISTIC
# SOCIAL WORK

*Humanistic Social Work –*
*The THIRD WAY*
*in Theory and Practice*

*Edition Entirely in English*

The
HUMANISTIC
SOCIAL WORK
Project

# TABLE OF CONTENTS

The
HUMANISTIC
SOCIAL WORK
Project

# CONTENTS

**Chapter 3. HUMANE AND SPIRITUAL QUALITIES OF THE PROFE-SSIONAL IN HUMANISTIC SOCIAL WORK PRACTICE  119**

# EDITION NOTICE

This book is the version entirely in English of the bilingual book with the same title, "Humane & Spiritual Qualities of the Professional in Humanistic Social Work: *Humanistic Social Work – The THIRD WAY in Theory and Practice*", published in November 2014, comprising, therefore, only its component in English language.

The present book is, so, a short version of the bilingual (English-Romanian) edition addressed with predilection to the English language readers.

This edition does not contain new elements of content and meaning, therefore is not recommended to be purchased by the English language readers who had read or purchased the bilingual version.

The
HUMANISTIC
SOCIAL WORK
Project

# FOREWORD

This book is a new apparition in a series of works, in print and/ or electronic form, dedicated to the professional, the practitioner, in humanistic social work. The emphasis is on its humane qualities, roles and behaviors, starting from the thesis that the humanistic social work axiology considers the psychological-humane resources, including the psychological-humane resources of the professional, expressed in humane and spiritual qualities, one of the main factors for the psychological rehabilitation and social re-integration of the persons in suffering and/ or difficulty, of the clients.

The inclusion in the work of a section dedicated to the presentation of *The HUMANISTIC SOCIAL WORK Project* is justified, on the one hand, by the fact that the book it is part of this project, of promoting and theorizing the express humanistic values and methods in social work practice, and, on the other hand, by the fact that the humane and spiritual qualities of the professional in social work, being a topic of utmost importance which the specialized literature does not give the due weight, requires even the framework of a project, which, through the values and priorities that it promotes, to propose a displacement from the simplistic, traditional or structuralist-functionalist paradigms of representation the professional, the practitioner, towards a complex paradigm, humanistic stated and assumed, thus highlighting also a tendency of the contemporary curative social practices, of accentuation the importance of the spiritual and humane factors in achieving the performance and fulfilling the objectives centered simultaneously on rehabilitation but also on the sustainable changes (of the individuals and groups/ communities).

The HUMANISTIC SOCIAL WORK Project sustain, therefore, an innovative vision on the professional, focusing, primarily, on the importance of the humane psychological and behavioral traits, on the deep and authentic resources of the personality, born or acquired, on the professional's intrinsic personal qualities, even if it does not disregard the crucial importance of the instrumental and behavioral personal qualities, skills and competencies, the importance of the professional knowledge and intellectual training, the importance of the professional experience or of the practical, technical, methodological skills, abilities and competencies.

In this sense, the project is distinguished by its emphasis on the humane, psychological-spiritual qualities of the professional represented as HUMAN, as a person, as a human being with personality and soul, in the specific activities/ roles, whether these are carried out by the social worker or psychologist, by the manager or caregiver, particularizing itself, thus, in the concert of the specialized literature which focuses predominantly on the instrumental and behavioral qualities, skills, competencies of the professional (even these being studied, theorized and popularized through the application, almost exclusive, to the practice, activity of the social worker, placing in the background or neglecting the qualities, skills, competencies of the other professionals in the field, as the caregiver, psychologist etc.

Humanistic social work, as the third way in contemporary social work, argues, therefore, the necessity of a new optic and a new concept regarding the professional, its roles, behaviors and qualities, also by the fact that it extends the interest over all professionals, not limiting it to the social workers.

In the light of the main values and goals of the humanistic social work practice, the personality and behavior of each professional from a service or institution of social assistance/ work represents important conditions and factors in the process of rehabilitation/ integration, or in providing of some optimal humane conditions for the beneficiaries' comfort and happiness.

The subtitle *Humanistic Social Work - The THIRD WAY in Theory and Practice* puts also the problem of the humane and spiritual qualities of the professional in the contemporary philosophical-doctrinal debates, dominated, mainly, by the opposition between the traditional/ conventional social work and the critical/ radical social work, where the humanistic social work comes with *the third way.*

So, if traditional social work prioritizes qualities and behaviors of the professional such as mercy, compassion, physical and emotional care, and critical social work qualities and behaviors such as visionary, determination, creativity, humanistic social work, as the third way, takes them from the both sides, adapting them, but comes with many new qualities/ skills - the majority taken and adapted from the therapeutic, pedagogical and managerial practice of the humanistic orientation - thus promoting, for the professional from humanistic social work practice, qualities and behaviors related to a model of personality highly developed, spiritually, humanly and culturally.

In this paper, in The HUMANISTIC SOCIAL WORK Project framework, we concentrate on a number of qualities that we consider representative for the way in which we describe humanistic social work as the third way in contemporary social work, which have, as the main psychological-personal source, what we call *Humane Personality*, with three constitutional spheres: the psychological-ontological sphere, the axiological-moral/ prosocial sphere, and the motivational-energetical sphere. It is about qualities such as *Empathy* and *Compathy, Spiritual Welfare* and *Virtue, Happiness* and *Eudaimonic-Altruistic Energy/ Motivation, Personal Development, Humane Development* and *Humanity.*

Empathy and compathy, this core humane resources/ qualities, skills of the practitioner, is a necessity in humanistic social work practice, and should not miss to any person activating in the overall social welfare/ work system. Through empathy the worker's personality becomes sensitive to the sufferings and problems of the people in need, and, at the behavioral level, acquires agreeability, openness. Empathy is, also, a fundamental way of knowledge and representation/ evaluation of the customer and the environment in which it lives.

Through the empathetic and compathetic valences of the personality a worker from a residential institution for children, for example, can help to create a magical psychosocial and humane "universe" for satisfying the intimate, deep, empathetic personal needs, spiritual growth and education, emotional and moral development of the children.

We can, so, to consider, empathy and compathy, a benchmark of quality, and a necessary condition in the preparation, recruitment and evaluation of personnel.

Spiritual welfare, as state and latent resource, and virtue, as (spiritual) energy and active resource, are others crucial personality resources and qualities of the professional in humanistic social work practice.

So, spiritual development/ sensitivity and virtue, as professional's qualities, resources, energies and conducts, may be considered important factors in the activity effectiveness and achieving the specific objectives of practice, especially in the activities with children, elderly and persons with disabilities, in casework, in caring, education, and direct therapy/ intervention/ social work.

Likewise, the happiness and eudemonic-altruistic energy/ motivation is an essential humanistic resource of the professional, especially of the practitioner who works directly with the client. That is the reason why happiness and eudemonic-altruistic energy/ motivation, as professional's qualities, resources, energies and conducts, may be considered crucial factors in the activity effectiveness and achieving the specific objectives of practice, mainly in casework, in caring, education, and therapy, in the activities with children, elderly and persons with disabilities, in the activities with sick people, and other.

The activity of the professional in humanistic social work/ welfare "system" cannot be conceived also without qualities such as personal development, humane development and humanity - very important resources and crucial factors of the activity effectiveness and achieving the objectives with almost all categories of clients and social problems, described in humanistic social work as *humane* problems, carried out by almost all categories of personnel.

These qualities are, but, indispensable, especially, for the professionals who, through their work, involves broad categories of problems and customers, or having responsibilities of strategy, planning, supervision, management or training. The personal development, humane development and humanity confers to manager, strategist, educator and supervisor characteristics which helps to operate, efficiently and at the same time, *both with the soul and with the mind.*

December 2014

*Petru Stefaroi*

# BRIEF PRESENTATION (SUMMARY) OF THE BOOK

For those who do not intend, or do not have enough time to read the entire book, we offer here a brief presentation, a summary, where are introduced some of the most important ideas, elements and fragments, with mention that it does not pretend to cover the whole range of issues, or the entire structure of the text.

The present book contains mainly three parts.

In the **PART I** is presented **THE *HUMANISTIC SOCIAL WORK PROJECT*** - our initiative, started in 2009, with the assumed aim to enhance the effective presence of the humanistic values, theories and practices in contemporary social work, a theoretical, axiological and methodological framework, a heuristic laboratory, a philosophical, scientific and professional forum wherein it can be set, what could be called, *the theory, axiology and methodology of the **Humanistic** Social Work*.

The project's intentions and elements are presented, in this book, in ten sections, respectively: *1. The Main Aim of the Project and The Ways of Promoting; 2. Establishing and Promoting the Humanistic Social Work as Concept, Paradigm, Philosophy/ Doctrine and Imposing as the Third Way in Theory and Method, Alongside Traditional/ Conventional Social Work and Critical/ Radical Social Work; 3. Establishing and promoting the basic/ support and specific theory/ theories of humanistic social work; 4. Promoting and Developing a Humanistic Perspective and Approach on the Social Problems: Social Problems as Human Problems; 5. Promoting and Developing a Humanistic Representation and Approach of the Client; 6. Promoting a Humanistic Perspective on the Policies, Activities and Practices of the Authorities, Services and*

*Institutions; 7. Establishing and Promoting the Specific and Core Mission, Values, Objectives and Principles of the Humanistic Social Work Practice; 8. Establishing and Promoting the Humanistic Social Work Methodology and Methods in Practice; 9. Establishing and Promoting an Express Humanistic Code of Ethics in Practice; 10. Promoting and Developing a Humanistic Perspective on the Practitioner's Personality, Behavior and Activity; Highlighting the Importance of the Humane and Spiritual Qualities of the Professional as Core Resource of Practice.*

So, one of the most important goal of the project is to circumscribe, philosophically and doctrinally, the *Humanistic Social Work* as *concept, theory* and *methodology*, and promoting, alongside *Traditional/ Conventional Social Work* and *Radical/ Critical Social Work*, alongside their theories and methods, as THE THIRD WAY in contemporary social work theory and practice, but also to promote and development a humanistic perspective on the practitioner's personality, behavior and activity in social work, highlighting the importance of the humane and spiritual qualities of the professional as core resource of practice.


**PART II, HUMANE AND SPIRITUAL QUALITIES OF THE PROFESSIONAL IN HUMANISTIC SOCIAL WORK** is the basic body of the paper, and is composed predominantly of free chapters.

The text represents a new step in our effort to contribute at the development of the humanistic social work theory and methodology, with special attention paid to the professional/ practitioner (social worker, caregiver, psychologist, etc.), to his psychological-spiritual and humane qualities and conducts in practice.

So, from a postmodern and post-postmodern position, the *humanistic social work way* proposes a new vision and approach on the professional and his personal (psychological, behavioral) qualities. It is a prioritization of the humane and spiritual qualities, such as empathy and compathy, spiritual welfare and virtue, happiness and eudemonic-altruistic energy/ motivation, personal development, human development and humanity - qualities and conducts analytically addressed in this section of the book.

Because, in practice (casework, caring, therapy, education etc.), between the practitioner's personality and the client's personality is established a high degree of emotional, empathetic, human, spiritual congruence, the cultivation, promotion of the spiritual and humane values of the professional's personality, as well as the achievement of a consistent specific literature is an important theoretical concern – topic/ theme approached, with predilection, in the humanistic social work theory and methodology framework.

**Chapter 1, *Humanistic Social Work - The Third Way in Social Work Theory and Practice*,** is devoted to present, theoretically, the concept, doctrine and specific of humanistic social work, with emphasis on its main sources, values, theories, practices and methods, to circumscribe, philosophically and doctrinally, Humanistic Social Work as *the third way*, alongside Traditional/ Conventional Social Work and Radical/ Critical Social Work, in the contemporary social work practice and theory, with the assumed claim to imposing even as dominant in the future.

Through the imposing of the concept-system "humanistic social work" is marks the transition into a new phase, where the humanistic orientation enhances and enriches their actual presence in social work theory, practice and policy, and becomes more than an occasional association of terms - a system-concept, a strong and unitary theory, and a distinct theoretical and methodological paradigm/ way of social work and social welfare

As philosophy and theory, humanistic social work is, yet, now, a conglomerate of theories, paradigms, orientations, but which have some crucial ideas as vectors: the person/ client as human being, with sentiments, soul, personality, desires, sufferings, needs of love, needs of happiness and accomplishments, emphasis on personality, the human relationships and micro-community as basic resources of practice, positive, optimistic and appreciative expectation in practice, person-centred and community-centred approach in evaluation and intervention, concentration on the future and not on the past, the human rights, social justice, a humanistic perspective on the practitioner and his conducts in practice.

*Humanism*, with its phenomenological and existentialist philosophical foundations, through all its artistic, social, philosophical, scientific, ideological, political, educational dimensions, manifestations and concerns, through the multitude of themes and meanings by which it was consecrated, as system or mode of thought and action where prevails the human interests, the human values and dignity, as variety of ethical theories and practices that emphasize the human fulfillment through knowledge and social development, focusing on the person/

individual/ being/ self, centering on the person's resources, the self-determination, human solidarity, humanity, human sensitivity, philanthropy, happiness, promoting the person's welfare, through the constitutional concern for researching the human being, his nature, essence, condition, through the interest for promoting of some great general human values and ideals in the evolution and development of society, through the interest for change and new, for truth, beautiful, good, represents the central foundation and essential source of the social work's theory and practice, in general, the more of the humanistic social work theory and practice.

The "humanistic social work" concept attempts to meets and organize, epistemological-methodological, the humanistic theory and methodology from the contemporary social work, into system, giving both a unitary theoretical and methodological framework and a forum for debate and professional or scientific innovation. Personal and socio-human development, participation, action, attachment, empathy and happiness theories, appreciative methods, humanistic psychotherapies and existential analysis are the theoretical and methodological bases of the policy and practice of the third way/ orientation in social work and social welfare.

A key concept and value of the humanistic social work theory and methodology is *human being*. The professional-client interaction is actually an inter-human relationship between two or more beings, with personality and soul, and, therefore, the success of intervention is crucial determined by its human nature and quality and not just by the economic resources or the used technology.

Empowerment is one of the most important means but also aim of practice in humanistic social work, aim achieved mainly through re-humanization, re-spiritualization and re-enlightenment of the individual and community – starting from the idea that, in the most part, the social issues and situations of difficulty have as main explanation a pronounced deficit of humanism, spirituality and culture in the people's personality or in the socio-human communities.

In this perspective the core mission and task of the humanistic social work practice would be to promote a compathetic attitude in the practitioner-client relationship, through creating a socio-human environment based on empathy, love and humanity, by humanizing the community, by changing the customers and communities through spiritual empowerment, personal/ community development, and responsibility, starting from the person/ community's right to happiness and well-being, but also from their right to dignity and self-determination.

To this end, one of the most important role of the professional in humanistic social work is to enable, with his humane and spiritual qualities, with his socio-human and professional experience and knowledge, with humane conducts, the client, a person or community, to become capable of coping with the crisis situations, with the difficult situations which can appears any time.

In agreement with the two main established theoretical-axiological meanings of the humanistic orientation, respectively, on the one hand, regarding the general human condition, the idea of ancestral human unity and solidarity, and, on the other hand, regarding the intrinsic resources and capacities of the individual, as person, of affirmation, self-actualization, self-determination, personal achievement and development, on can speak, consequently, of two relatively distinct theories, forms, ways of humanistic social work, ie *the solidarist-humanistic social work* and the *positive-humanistic social work*.

**The Chapter 2, *Humane Personality And Soul – Personal-Psychological Sources of the Professional's Humane and Spiritual Qualities*,** shows what might be called, in our view, the personal-psychological sources of the professional's humane and spiritual qualities in humanistic social work practice, mainly the soul (as the most important component of the psychological-ontological sphere of the humane personality), with the sub-spheres: *affective (social) soul, spiritual soul* (mystical, playful, aesthetic, moral, intellectual) and *humane soul*. It is not negligible nor the role of the axiological-moral/prosocial sphere, or of the motivational-energetical sphere.

Yet, the humane and spiritual qualities, traits, or resources, such as empathy, virtue, spirituality, happiness, humanity, and more, are expressions of some personal constructs of a maximum complexity, generated by the existence of a mega-system that exceeds both the ontological and psychological sphere, involving the person as a whole, represented in the ancestral and socio-cultural context, dimensions projected mostly in what, in the paper, we call the humane personality.

Ultimately, the personality model of the professional in humanistic social work, capable of generating qualities such as empathy, virtue, spirituality, happiness, humanity, altruism, is the humane personality that combines the global personality developed to a higher level with the personality so structured that determines effective professional conducts both in the objectives regarding the personal empowerment and social integration, and also in the objectives regarding the reduction of the client's suffering, or of happiness.

To this end, the theoretical model of personality that we use in this paper, developed by us, respectively humanist-ontopersonological, wherein the soul has the central role, has been used before in other our paper appearances, respectively in the articles (titles translated in English): "Humanistic Perspective on Customer in Social Work", no. 1-2, 2009, "Socio-Affective Development Disorders of Institutionalized Child. From the Survival Objective towards the Happiness Objective in Social Work for Children", no. 1-2, 2008, published in *Social Work Review* (Faculty of Sociology and Social Work - University of Bucharest), by Polirom Publishing House, also in the book "Happiness Theory in Social Work: From Care Management to Happiness Management" , Lumen Publishing House, 2009, Romania.

Aspects of this theory we will present therefore in this paper, considering the soul as the central ontoformation of the humane personality, the most important source of the practitioner's humane and spiritual qualities in humanistic social work practice.

The term *humane personality* which we use, conventionally, in the paper refers mainly to a set of onto-formations, such as soul, humane self, humane consciousness, humane character, and other - structural onto-psychological and intellectual sources of the person's humane and spiritual qualities, as well as at the humanistic orientation, quality, the overall humane valence, dimension of the global personality, meaning kindness, goodness, altruism, personality opened to the overall manhood jouissance, increased sensitivity towards the other's suffering/ tragedy - itself, but also emergent resource of empowerment, wellbeing and happiness for the people from ambience; both being foundations and explanations of the professional's humane and spiritual qualities, of its humane, altruistic, prosocial behavior in humanistic social work.

Therefore, the complex and complete meaning of the concept *humane personality* includes the both approaches, determining superior valences (qualities/ resources) of the person/ personality/ conduct, such as spirituality, virtue, humanity, authentic happiness, etc. As sphere, includes at least the following sub-spheres: psychological-ontological; motivational-eudaimonical sphere, and axiological-moral/ prosocial.

Starting from the main topic of the book, focused on the humane and spiritual qualities of the professional in humanistic social work practice, such as empathy and compathy, spiritual welfare and virtue, happiness and eudemonic-altruistic energy/ motivation, personal development, humane development and humanity, we consider the following:

1. the psychological-ontological sphere of the humane personality, especially the soul, has the main role in determining the empathy, compathy and spiritual welfare, spirituality,

2. the motivational-eudaimonical sphere has the main role in determining the happiness and eudemonic-altruistic energy/ motivation, and

3. the axiological-moral/ prosocial sphere has the main role in determining qualities of the person/ professional such as personal development, humane development and humanity, humanness.

All in the context in which every trait, quality, resource of the personality is also an effect of system, and gains significance only in behavioral context.

So, in a complex, humanistic view, the humane and spiritual qualities of the professional are not mere expressions of the emotional and spiritual development, of the affective soul, of the spiritual and humane spheres, but rather expressions of the general cultural development, of the existence of certain skills or inclinations, of the character development, or of the eudemonic-spiritual and eudaimonic-prosocial spheres, and, not least, of the development of personality as a whole, through its humane/ humanistic orientation/ dimension, as a personality developed at a higher level, closer to the condition of human being of the person, as cultural, rational, spiritual and autonomous existence with its characteristic attributes - morality, virtue sociality, spirituality, personal development, adaptability and socio-human efficiency, as well as personality structured, through the soul, ego, conscience, character, motivation, skills, etc., so that determines conducts oriented to the welfare of the other, of the generalized other, of the community, humanity, and dominant traits, qualities such as empathy, altruism, generosity, kindness, etc.

Ultimately, the model of personality of the professional in humanistic social work, capable of generating qualities such as empathy, virtue, spirituality, happiness, humanity, altruism, is the humane personality that combines the global personality developed to a higher level with the personality so structured that determines effective professional conducts both in the objectives regarding the personal empowerment and social integration, but also in the ones of diminishing the client's suffering, or of happiness.

**In the Chapter 3,** *Humane and Spiritual Qualities of The Professional in Humanistic Social Work Practice* - effectively is reached the content of the topic proposed by the book's main title, approaching so the theme regarding the humane and spiritual qualities of the professional starting from the category of "humane personality of the professional", and insisting on the necessity to define it in connection with the spiritual-humanistic mode/ way of representation and approach of the customer.

In practice, in case work, in caring and education in a residential institution, the psychological-spiritual and humane qualities of the professional, respectively empathy and compathy, spiritual welfare and virtue, happiness and eudemonic-altruistic energy/ motivation, personal development, humane development and humanity, approached, in the chapter, through reporting to criteria of activity effectiveness and achieving the objectives, are of great importance also in the goal regarding the organizational's congruence, consistency, unity and functionality.

In the same chapter is trying a presentation of the most important humane and spiritual qualities of the social worker, of the psychologist, of the caregiver, the manager, the supervisor, and of others social work professionals in the humanistic social work/ welfare "system", especially in child and family social work/ welfare, in the care activities, in residential institutions, etc.

*Empathy* and *compathy, spiritual welfare* and *virtue, happiness* and *eudemonic-altruistic energy/ motivation, personal development, human development* and *humanity* are, after our opinion, the most important qualities of the professional in any paradigm of social work, but in humanistic social work has a crucial role.

Through empathy, spirituality, happiness and humanity the worker's personality becomes sensitive to the sufferings and problems of the people in need, and, at the behavioral level, acquires agreeability, tolerance, altruism, openness. The ability to feel the enjoyment (desire, suffering) of the other, the ability to think and experience what another person thinks and feels, the ability to really put in another place, to see the world as other person see it, the personal motivation oriented towards the other, sympathetic projection of the self, emotional-affective fusion, sympathetic intuition, introjection, transitivism, intro-pathy, sympathy, identification with the other, transfer, etc. the worker acquires access to the customer's personality and obtains an effective method/ tool of therapeutic change. These are also a fundamental way of knowing the customer and the environment where he lives.

In institutions the professional-client inter-empathy has a undeniable curative function. The care organization is a network of inter-empathies where, especially in children's institutions, the profe-ssional's personality can have a vital educational function. The professional's personality interacts with all its physical, psychological, social, cultural, moral level and features.

To this end the social care organization/ institution is defined also by the personalities that made it, including the professionals' persona-lities, with the three dimensions: affective, cognitive and spiritual. So, the socio-affective phenomena are, in fact, relationships, interactions, compathies between the affective spheres of the persons, while the cognitive and spiritual phenomena are processes, inter alia, between its spiritual spheres and/ or projective selves.

Through the spiritual and prosocial valences of the humane personality a professional from a residential institution for children, elders, persons with disabilities, etc., can help to create a magical psychosocial and cultural "universe" for satisfying their intimate, deep, human needs, for satisfying their needs of spiritual growth and equilibration, of happiness, for satisfying their needs, especially for children, of emotional, social and moral development.

The institution, even it is the last solution for placement, is for the child, however, the place where is built the human-ontological foundations of its personality, is the environment where the child is feed with spiritual and moral energy, is the existential magic framework of training, existence and manifestation of his personality, of its happiness and soulful/ personal fulfillment.

This is the reason why the role of the psychological-spiritual and humane qualities of the professionals is so important, and must to be accentuated, promoted and cultivated, in practice and literature.

In general, with his qualities, knowledge, experience, soul, personality and behavior the social worker operates for the formation and development of the client's humane and prosocial personality, for formation and development of his optimistic and prosocial attitudes, expressed in conducts and qualities of personality as adaptability, conscientiousness, accountability, balance, diligence, happiness, virtue - qualities and conducts of the personality that would facilitates the personal and social rehabilitation of the client in humanistic social work/ welfare "system".

Also, regarding the behavior, activity and objectives of the psychologist in humanistic social work, the psychological, spiritual and humane qualities play a crucial role, these are, actually, some inexhaustible resources, but mostly a therapeutic mobiles, with which the humanistic psychologist achieves their specific objectives in the multidisciplinary team. In this regard, the psychologist's personality or its spiritual qualities shall be described in terms of complex personality, exceptional spiritual traits, soul, empathy, spiritual welfare and happiness, spiritual/ humane sensitivity, agreeableness, charisma, culture and humane intelligence.

Regarding the psychological-spiritual and humane qualities of the caregiver or of the other workers directly being in connection with the clients, among the qualities brought to attention in this paper, namely empathy and compathy, spiritual welfare and virtue, happiness and eudemonic-altruistic energy and motivation, personal development, human development and humanity, probably spiritual welfare and virtue, happiness and eudaimonic-altruistic energy and motivation, empathy and compathy are further required.

Instead, for the manager, strategist and supervisor, engaged especially in leadership, planning, monitoring and mentoring activities, are useful, especially, qualities such as personal development, human development and humanity. The personal, human development and humanity anyway encompasses also the others, and confers to managers, supervisor's personality and behavior those characteristics which help to operate both with the soul and with the mind, even if would be perfect as the manager, strategist and supervisor to meet all the psycho-spiritual and humane qualities promoted by humanistic social work theory, axiology and methodology.

If there is an area of practice where are required, without exception, all the humane and spiritual qualities and resources of the professional's personality and conduct, then that area is the child and family social work. In this sense, the professional in family and child humanistic social work, is not a mere functionary which identify, bureaucratically, some malfunctions and tries to solve them in order of a merely technical recovery, simple restoration of the original family functioning, but seeks to identify also the human, spiritual, cultural, moral problems facing the family members.

The professional's personality and its psychological-spiritual and humane qualities represents, for this purpose, the means, the essential professional resource that can facilitate the achievement of the objectives in practice in child and family humanistic social work.

The professional's humanistic activity, its psychological-spiritual qualities and humane quality and behavior, can facilitate the family change, can humanize the troubled social relationships, the dehu-manized, dysfunctional micro-community, the moral, psychological damaged people, in difficulty, suffering, conflict, under-development, reaching so to perform the specific mission, to determine the family changes regarding his moral and human climate.

In this process the humanistic practitioner is involved with whole its self, soul, intellect and experience, in the complex assembly of relationships, connections, conflicts, attachments, inter-empathies, compathies, feelings, passions, loves, projects, dramas of the family group with problems, detecting the dysfunctions, problems, under-developments, anomalies, building the diagnostic by an etiology and phenomenology of morale and human type, focusing, therefore, on *highlighting the dysfunctions from the social/ human relationships level,* the intervention aiming *to convert them,* by means of the knowledge, experiences, humane personality, soul, and psychological-spiritual qualities of the professionals from the team intervention, in *humane and moral relationships,* determining improvements, impressive qualitative changes at the family level as a whole, as well at the level of each member of the family - the transformative process evolving in cascade, involving the humanizing sub-processes at all levels, eliminating many family dysfunctions, disorders, problems, member's sufferings - the new created family climate being defined by qualifiers such as harmony, morality, solidarity, altruism, compathy, responsibility, cooperation, etc. This climate will imposes, ultimately, as an important curative solution for many family problems.

The **PART III** of the book, **IDEAS, FRAGMENTS, ELEMENTS OF SOME NEW TEXTS (in working) IN THE** *HUMANISTIC SOCIAL WORK* **PROJECT,** includes three works, under preparation, to whom is working to appear, in the near future, within the project, respectively "Humanistic Social Work: *The Third Way in Social Work Theory and Practice*", "Humanistic Social Work Practice" and "Humanistic Social Work: *Humane Personality and Humane Relationships – Basic Resources of Practice*".

One of the main ideas highlighted in this works is the fact that, regardless of the specific and nature of the object of intervention, humanistic social work use these unlimited and miraculous resources: *the humane personality* (of the client, and of the professional) and *the humane relationships (in the* therapeutic processes, and in communities).

That is the reason why its theory and methodology operates with concepts like human being, soul, person, empathy, compathy, personal development, spirituality, culture, socio-human context, micro-community, solidarity, etc., especially when aims objectives at the family, organizational or community level.

The works starts from the finding that, at a first glance, social work, as theory, is dominated by two, relatively opposed, major ways, forces, orientations, paradigms, namely Traditional/ Conventional Social Work and Critical/ Radical Social Work

But, major social, political and economic events have strongly shaken the ontological and ideological foundation of the Traditional/ Conventional Social Work (the economic crisis), and of the Critical/ Radical Social Work (the anti-communist revolutions).

Such, has been greatly affected the policies/ practices of helping the vulnerable groups, individuals, people in need through welfare state mechanisms and social solidarity, within the capitalist society, promoted by Traditional/ Conventional Social Work, and the projects of some radical structural changes, the aspirations to build a better society, without oppression, social injustice, inequality, discrimination and poverty, especially through social and political reforms and progress, promoted by Critical/ Radical/ Progressive Social Work.

In this context, the necessity of a new approach in social work, with emphasis on the resources, theories and practices of empowerment (persons and communities) and empathy (as means of socio-human solidarity and therapeutic relationship), became more than obvious. So, in a subtle manner, gradually, seems to advance, with increasing force, the *humanistic orientation* and its logical expression: Humanistic Social Work - syntagma, philosophy, theory and methodology which are in process of establishing, and remains to be seen whether it will get to sit alongside Traditional/ Conventional Social Work and Critical/ Radical/ Progressive Social Work, alongside their theories and methods, and especially if it will imposes, in a coherent and consistent way, in the current practice of the professionals and agencies.

The process is closely related to the offensive of humanistic psychology and psychotherapy, on the one hand, and micro-sociology, humanistic sociology, humanistic management, education, etc., on the other hand. All in the context designed by the phenomenology, existentialism and postmodernism/ post-postmodernism thought in the social theory and practice areas.

In this context, the abundance, in contemporary social work, of the concepts and theories, methods and techniques from humanistic psychology and psychotherapy, humanistic sociology and micro-sociology, humanistic management and education, justify the observation that we can be, already, in the presence of a ***third way*** *in social work*, with almost certain perspectives to become dominant in the future.

Explanation is found in the fact that humanistic social work incorporates concepts and methods from the two established stances, but also brings many new elements, according to the new social, human, economic, cultural realities and trends, and the new achieve-

ments in science and practice. In this way, in addition, it can be stated that humanistic social work could become one of the most important doctrinal/ methodological solution for many social and human problems at the beginning of the third millennium.

So, the *humanistic social work* concept comes as a solution, a third way in theory and methodology, to keep what is valid in the two ways, especially the interest for person from traditional social work, and the interest for change from radical/ critical social work, and try to organize altogether, epistemologically and methodologically, into system, giving both a unitary theoretical and methodological frame-work, and a forum for debate and professional or scientific innovation.

The personal and socio-human development theories, attachment, empathy and happiness theories, on the one hand, and the humanistic psychotherapies, humanistic casework and case management, appre-ciative methods and balance method, on the other hand, are, in our opinion, largely, the theoretical and methodological bases of the policy and practice of the third way/ orientation in the contemporary social work and social welfare.

Between the crucial values of the humanistic social work practice are social justice; personal and human development of the customers: the complexity of the client's personality, and of the client system; methodological flexibility; evidence-based practice; valorization of the client's creativity, freedom and resources; development of the self, and the capitalization of spiritual potential; the priority of the client's interests, feelings and values; spiritual well-being and development of the client and community; human development, empowerment and self-determination of the person / client and community; equality, solidarity, compathy; human relationships as humane relationships; the importance of the professional's personality, education, human qualities, conducts, value and principles in practice.


The paper ends with some **CONCLUSIVE CONSIDERATIONS**, where, amongst other things, it concludes the aspect that the humanistic social work theory, methodology and axiology does not promote a unilateral representation of the professional, of its personality and conduct, of its basic personal qualities in practice.

As suggests also the origins of the term *humanism*, in which to knowledge is granted a privileged role, closely linked to the idea of human rights, emancipation and affirmation, humanistic social work promotes so the scientific training, and, in conclusion, multilateral and complex, of the professional.

Therefore, the professional's personality, in the perspective of theory, axiology and methodology of humanistic social work, is a psychosocial and cultural construction of very high complexity, gathering, onto-genetically, the natural datum with the education/ training, the internal resources with the life and professional experience.

Referring to the *specific resources* of humanistic social work, in the last section of the book, it states the idea that if traditional social work is focused on the person in need  and/ or suffering, and critical/ radical social work on the social structure and system, humanistic social work locates some-where in the middle, her "place" being, so, the human relationships, especially the *humane* relationships, promoting, so, the solidarity, commitment, compathy, humanity, shared well-being and happiness.

For this purpose the work of professionals and services focuses on exploiting the resources from the micro-community level - families, organizations, neighborhoods, couples, institutions, putting in back-ground, without disregard, the resources from the macro-level, or the concerns for biological survival and strictly body care.

From this position, humanistic social work recognizes and promotes the importance of the resources and defining values of  critical/ radical social work and traditional social work, the community/ society and the human body, but prioritizes the importance of the personality/ soul and of the humane relationships, both as resources also as values and goals of the practice, thus tending to complete the complex area of the socio-human existence, structured on the three levels: individual, micro community, and society. This is also the reason why humanistic social work puts a great emphasis on the humane and psychological-spiritual qualities of professional.

In this mission the humanistic practitioner make an "insertion", an involvement, with whole its personal resources (self, soul, intellect, character, consciousness, experience), in the complex assembly of relationships, connections, conflicts, attachments, inter-empathies, compathies, feelings, passions, loves, projects, dramas, of the group with problems.

He detect the dysfunctions, problems, underdevelopments, anomalies, building the diagnostic panel by an etiology and phenomenology of existential-humanistic type, focusing, therefore, on highlighting the *dysfunctions from the social/human relations level*, the intervention aiming to convert them, by means of its knowledge, experiences, humane personality, soul, humane and spiritual qualities in *humane relationships*.

The change for better on the social/ human relationships level, transformed into *humane* relationships, will generate improvements, impressive qualitative changes, at the micro-community level as a whole, as well at the level of each person; the transformative processes evolving in cascade, involving humanizing sub-processes at all levels, eliminating, automatically, many dysfunctions, disorders, problems, sufferings.

*This environment will impose, ultimately, as a curative solution for many problems and difficult situations, and only to the extent that the professionals and social services manage to lead, to generate it, with their qualities, activities, measures, conducts, can sustain that they operates thoroughly and efficiently, and meet their specific mission, at least in the perspective of the humanistic social work theory and axiology.*

# PART I
# THE
# HUMANISTIC SOCIAL WORK
# PROJECT

The
**HUMANISTIC**
**SOCIAL WORK**
Project

# 1.
## THE MAIN AIM OF THE PROJECT
## AND THE WAYS OF PROMOTING

The HUMANISTIC SOCIAL WORK Project is an initiative with the assumed **aim** to enhance the effective presence of the humanistic values, theories and practices in social work, which usually are stated as fundamental and essential in different programs, strategies and policies but less present, in fact, in the specialized literature, in the faculties' curricula, or in the practice of professionals and services. To this end, the project is designed as a theoretical, axiological and methodological framework, a heuristic laboratory, a philosophical, scientific and professional forum in which it can be set what might be called the theory, axiology and methodology of humanistic social work.

The project's concept starts from the idea that humanistic social work is not, however, a distinctive form of social work/ welfare but rather an ontology/ epistemology, that generates a reaffirmation/ restatement of the fundamental/ constitutional humanistic values of social work, incorporating, in the same time, in a (relative) new coherent and unitary theory, all what penetrated in social work in the last decades from humanistic psychology and psychotherapy, microsociology and humanistic sociology, human rights philosophy/ movement, and, especially, what was established as humanistic method in the contemporary social work practice and literature.

The main **way** of promoting the objectives and elements of the project is the publication of articles and books, both in classic and electronic format. Appearances in the project can be, also, considered, preliminary of this series of books, our articles published in *Social Work Review* (Faculty of Sociology and Social Work - University of Bucharest), by Polirom Publishing House, respectively (titles translated in English): "Humanistic Paradigm of Social Work or Brief Introduction in Humanistic Social Work", no. 1, 2012, "Humanistic Perspective on Customer in Social Work", no. 1-2, 2009, "Socio-Affective Development Disorders of Institutionalized Child. From the Survival Objective towards the Happiness Objective in Social Work for Children", no. 1-2, 2008, and "Efficient Management Particularity in Social Work", no. 3, 2007.

In addition to these, important contribution in the project is, also, the book (title translated in English) "Happiness Theory in Social Work: From Care Management to Happiness Management", Lumen Publishing House, 2009.

But, the papers in which I succeed to present, in assumed and clearly way, the project's objectives and elements, to explain, including philosophically (values, principles, ethics, doctrine, etc.) the concept of humanistic social work, as *the third way* in contemporary social work theory and practice, are the series of books "Calitati psihologic-sufletesti ale profesionistului in asistenta sociala umanista" (2013), and "Calitati psihologic-sufletesti ale profesionistului in asistenta sociala umanista – The HUMANISTIC SOCIAL WORK Project: Humanistic Social Work – The Third Way in Theory and Practice" (2014), CreateSpace, Charleston SC, Amazon.com Company, USA; series continued to the present paper.

Also, a crucial contribution in shaping the system of values, theories and methods of humanistic social work, and imposing the project as a framework for promotion and publication have had a series of works published in electronic format, grouped and published, the most significant, in three collections, namely: "Psychology and Humanistic Social Work Electronic Collection", "Sociology and Humanistic Social Work Electronic Collection", and "Philosophy and Humanistic Social Work Electronic Collection".

Among these works we mention: "Humanistic Social Work Theories and Methods: Personality – Core Resource of Practice", and "Spiritual Qualities of the Professional in Humanistic Social Work Practice". The vast majority of works were taken and displayed by bookstores, libraries, Websites from the virtual space.

An important step in shaping and developing the Project is, also, represented by the realization of the work (title translated in English) "Humanistic Social Work: From Care and Survival to Happiness and Human Rehabilitation", draft book consists of about 200 pages, that participated in a competition for funding, organized by the Administration of the National Cultural Fund, in august 2010, Romania. Because this paper did not meet conditions for financing I decided, therefore, to sharing/ spread the ideas and content in a larger number of appearances, print and electronic, books and articles, which, also, appeared, some of them, until now, within the project.

## 2.
## ESTABLISHING AND PROMOTING THE *HUMANISTIC SOCIAL WORK* AS CONCEPT, PARADIGM AND PHILOSOPHY/ DOCTRINE, AND IMPOSING AS THE THIRD WAY, ALONGSIDE TRADITIONAL SOCIAL WORK AND CRITICAL SOCIAL WORK

Is not a easy work to delimit and establish the framework and the borders of a concept and paradigm, more so if it is about of a humanistic concept and paradigm, which, are known that, it is of immense complexity and vastness.

However, as highlights and Malcolm Payne, the humanistic paradigm is present in social work, but lacks a distinctive and express theory to impose it, to give him specific content. To this end, the humanistic social work theory and concept comes to fill this gap.

*Most social work practice is humanistic, but this is usually not made explicit or explored fully in social work education or practice. Therefore, I see this book as coloring in a pencil sketch we made some time ago that we now want to turn into an oil painting. We were happy with the sketch; it gave us outlines of how we might see and understand the world. But without the oils, we cannot display it proudly as our contribution to understanding and living helpfully and lovingly among human beings (Payne, 2011, p. 1).*

Especially after the appearance of the book "Humanistic Social Work: Core Principles in Practice", by Malcolm Payne, in 2010/ 2011, the humanistic social work, as concept, theory and paradigm is, in obviously offensive.

The author links the humanistic social work concept, theory, paradigm and practice with some fundamental principles and values such as human rights, personal and spiritual development, creativity, accountability and social justice, identifying as the main theoretical and methodological sources/ models the humanistic and phenomenological thinking, philosophy of existence/ (human) being, existential-humanistic psychology/ psychotherapy, transpersonal psychology, social constructivism and microsociology. A key term of the humanistic social work concept and philosophy is the *human being*.

I, in the article "Humanistic Perspective on Customer in Social Work" (*Social Work Review*, no. 1-2, 2009, Polirom Publishing House), have summarized the concept "humanistic social work" putting in the foreground the humanistic representation/ approach of the client and the professional. I emphasized that the core aspect of the humanistic social work paradigm, theory and practice is determined by the way/ mode (humanistic) are represented the client and professional, considering the humane qualities/ resources of the client and professional the critical epistemological and methodological value of the this type of social work. We developed the humanistic social work paradigm, concept and theory in the article "Humanistic Paradigm of Social Work or Brief Introduction in Humanistic Social Work", appeared in the 2012, no.1, the same publication.

So, one of the most important goal of the project is to circumscribe, philosophically and doctrinally, the humanistic social work as concept, theory, methodology and practice. At first sight, the contemporary social work is dominated by two, relatively opposed, major ways, forces, orientations, paradigms, namely traditional/ conventional social work and critical/ radical social work. but, major social, political and economic events have strongly shaken the ontological and ideological foundation of the Traditional Social Work (economic crisis), and of the Critical Social Work (anti-communist revolutions). Such, has been greatly affected the policies/ practices of helping the vulnerable groups, individuals, people in need through the welfare state mechanisms and social solidarity, within the capitalist society, promoted by Traditional Social Work, and the projects of some radical structural changes, the aspirations to build a better society, without oppression, social injustice, inequality, discrimination and poverty, especially through social and political reforms and progress, even revolution, promoted by Critical Social Work.

In this context, another orientation, in a subtle manner, gradually, seems to advance, with increasing force. It's about, therefore, the humanistic orientation and its logical expression: HUMANISTIC SOCIAL WORK - syntagma, philosophy, theory and methodology which are in process of establishing, and remains to be seen whether it will get to sit alongside Traditional Social Work and Radical Social Work, alongside their theories and methods, and especially if it will imposes, in a coherent way, in the current practice of the professionals and agencies, as THE THIRD WAY.

# 3.

# ESTABLISHING THE BASIC/ SUPPORT AND SPECIFIC THEORY/ THEORIES OF THE HUMANISTIC SOCIAL WORK

In fact, in the current practice, all forms and orientations of social work are found combined in various proportions and manners, determined by the philosophy of approach, ideology and the social policy, by the specific of problems, the used methods and by the pursued objectives.

This is the reason why it can affirm that the specific theory of humanistic social work is a conglomerate of theories, paradigms, orientations, but which have some crucial ideas as vectors: the person/ client as human being, with sentiments, soul, personality, desires, sufferings, needs of love, needs of happiness and accomplishments; emphasis on personality and compathetic micro-community as basic resources of practice; positive, optimistic and appreciative expectation in practice; person-centred and community-centred approach in evaluation and intervention; concentration on the future and not on the past; the human rights, social justice; a humanistic perspective on the practitioner and his conducts in practice.

Humanism, with all its philosophical, ethical, aesthetic and scientific dimensions, is, after Payne, the fundamental source of ideas and values for humanist social work. Starting from the value-concept of humanism, in concrete, the author makes reference, as our interpretation, at three major theoretical areas, as main sources for the humanist social work theory, axiology, methodology and practice, respectively philosophy (especially phenomenology and existentialism), psychology/ psychotherapy (especially the humanistic orientation) and sociology (especially microsociology).

The theories of personality (development) and (human) being, empathy theory, attachment theory and happiness theory are, according to our point of view, among the most important theoretical sources/ grounds and theories of the of humanistic social work.

The Theories of Personality (development) and (human) Being in humanistic social work are a theoretical model and support for representing both the client and the worker as human beings, with personality, soul, character, sensibility and empathy, and not as simple individuals being in a simple social and professional interaction.

Empathy Theory is a formative instrument used by the professionals in achieving the specific objectives, mainly in the human rehabilitation and social empowerment of the client. The practitioner-client proactive empathetic relationship is, in fact, a framework for transfer, a subtle lane that the professional uses, intentionally and professionally, for solving the problem.

Happiness Theory is based on the assumption that efficiency and personal/ professional/ social adaptation is closely related to the degree of happiness of the individuals and communities. Psychological-spiritual well-being is a factor of energy and self-development/ auto-nomy - so reducing the degree of social vulnerability and the likelihood to becoming a client of the social services.

Attachment Theory theorizes the importance of the affection process and phenomena in social relationships and coexistence, especially regarding the role of child-parent attachment relationship in the formation of o balanced and adaptive personality of the child. In child care institutions is interesting to see the role of attachment also in the quality of the human relationships between the care professionals, between the professionals and children, etc.

# 4.

# PROMOTING AND DEVELOPING A HUMANISTIC PERSPECTIVE AND APPROACH ON THE SOCIAL PROBLEMS. SOCIAL PROBLEMS AS *HUMAN* PROBLEMS

In humanistic social work so called social problems are in fact human, or socio-human problems. The persons involved in relationships and communities are not simple social elements of the social organizations, they have personalities, souls, feelings, dramas, sufferings. Their problems are, so, not of social order but of human order.

In this end, the human suffering, unhappiness, personal failure, loss, the dehumanization of the individual and community, the emotional drama and great collective tragedies, the disasters with significant human impact, the personal/ community underdevelopment are among the central phenomena and categories of, what might be called in scientific terms, the problems and object of intervention in humanistic social work practice.

The human suffering, unhappiness, personal failure, maladjustment, marginalization, social vulnerability are often related to a human/ socio-human problem, to a human difficult situation, and, often, the normalization cannot be achieved without its elimination or limitation.

Problem and object of intervention, in humanistic social work, are also the lack of personal fulfillment, the existential issues, the lack of humanity and empathy/ compathy, of morality, the dehumanization of the individual, etc.

The practitioners, in their daily professional activity, interact with unmet, professional or personal, individuals, who have failed or have deviated from the optimal way to achieve the personal, professional and social goals, who daily live chronic dissatisfaction and personal dramas.

So, the loss, separation, uprooting, loneliness, poverty, promiscuity, discrimination, marginalization are social and personal issues. with great personal and social impact, but are also ontological or humane problems. Each of these can be considered part of what, we might call, the phenomenon or process of dehumanization, human degradation of the individuals and communities.

The communities where predominate the undeveloped (human/ personal/ moral) individuals - selfish, individualistic, concerned only on the personal benefit - are aprioristic prone to problems.

In the humanistic paradigm of social work the vulnerability, difficult situation of the person is so associated, mainly, with the delays and disorders of personal and human development, with the ontological inconsistency and poor quality of the interpersonal relationships, with degradation of the values systems (moral, cultural, etc.) of the community and organizations.

Any social group, community or organization is also an empathetic community. Therefore, many human suffering, tragedy or social problems are rooted in its underdevelopment, in weaknesses or very serious compathetic problems. The knowledge of this aspect by the social workers is a necessity and, moreover, the compathy, empathetic community, the system of human/ humane relationships, of sympathies and empathies can be very effective tools for change, improvement, normalization.

# 5.

# PROMOTING AND DEVELOPING A HUMANISTIC REPRESENTATION AND APPROACH OF THE CLIENT

The humanistic theories represent the client as *human* being, as soul, subject of silent suffering and happiness, and not only as a neutral individual of a social system, or humble beneficiaries of the community's services. So, the humanistic theories convert the client from individual in person, in human being, in I, in subject, soul.

In accordance with the *principles of humanistic psychology* each healthy person, as client, has the potential capacity to recover, to fulfill as person, to be happy, in human, social and spiritual terms, but everything depends, mainly, of its internal activism, of willingness to self-change or accomplishment, but, also, of the identification and using his internal resources, including with the professional aid.

The (humanistic) representation of the client in humanistic social work starts from the five basic beliefs of humanistic psychology, respectively:

- humans supersede the sum of their parts;

- persons have their existence in a uniquely human context;

- they are aware of being aware (conscious);

- they have free will;

- every normal person are intentional about goals and personal achievement.

In the light of these principles, the humanistic perspective on the customer in humanistic social work involves taking into account its potential capacity to recover, to fulfill as person, to be happy, taking into account its aesthetic, playful, epistemological and mystical needs. Namely, the spiritual needs.

Meeting and development the spiritual needs, the development of the spiritual personality is one of the most effective methods/ ways for the personal development of the customer, and enhance the perspective of personal/ social empowerment, recovery, reintegration, regardless of the education level, origin, age or types of social/ human problems.

Humanistic social work, as the third way in contemporary social work, takes over from traditional social work the care for the client as person, being, soul, personality and focus on the compathetic, concrete context/ environment where he lives, while, from the critical/ radical social work the interest for social/ human progress and change.

In a complex representation and approach of the client, in the first case humanistic social work operates mainly with the concept of empathy, while in the second case with the concept of empowerment. The two terms, empathy and empowerment, having a constitutional role in the practice of the professional (social worker, caregiver, therapist etc.) humanistic social work.

# 6.
# PROMOTING A HUMANISTIC PERSPECTIVE
# ON THE POLICIES, ACTIVITIES AND PRACTICES
# OF THE AUTHORITIES,
# SERVICES AND INSTITUTIONS

As is well known, social work is, theoretically and ideologically, based on the resources of the social and human sciences, of philosophy and other areas of the science and practice, but is also much conditioned of the political ideas, of the different ideologies from the history or from the present. This is one of the reasons why the theory and practice of social work, the activity of the services and institutions, are so complex and full of dichotomies and doctrinal or methodological contradictions, taking, so, from these the majority ideas and tools of practice, but also and the theoretical/ doctrinal debates, regarding the relationships between individual and society, freedom and responsibility, matter and spirit, structure and element, individualism and solidarity, stagnation and change (through evolution/ progress vs. revolution), etc.

Practically, largely, the ideas for strategies, decisions and practice of the social work services and institution coming from behind or from other areas of knowledge and practice, assimilating them, usually afterwards, in a specific manner, and adapt them to the proper purpose, mission and methods. Thus, these determine the specific politics and methodology of social work authorities to include orientations, ways, theories from the whole areas of contemporary ideologies, philosophies and socio-human sciences: conservator, socialist, liberal, feminist, phenomenologist, existentialist, post-modern, structuralist, behaviorist, psychosocial, cognitivist, holist, functionalist, criticist, traditionalist, radical, humanist, etc.

Yet, as we pointed out, at a first glance, social work, as ideology, theory and practice, is dominated by two, relatively opposed, major ways, forces, orientations, namely *Traditional or Conventional* Social Work and *Radical or Critical* Social Work. In an ideological and political view the Traditional or Conventional Social Work can be associated with the conservatorist orientation from politics, with the classical capitalism, whereas the Radical and Critical Social Work can be associated with the, so called, progressive policies and the new, critical, tendencies of the capitalist society, especially with the leftist orientation of policy.

The Traditional Social Work is the starting point in any theoretical and ideological discussion regarding the values, mission and methods of the social work services and institutions, for the simple reason that it is the first and original form, but also because it provides the fundamental system of values and purposes of the social work/ welfare practice. Human/ social solidarity, redistribution, sensibility and caring for the other's welfare are universal values and objectives of the social work, anytime and anywhere. But, the Traditional Social Work is accused of an attitude of condescension and contempt towards its clients, being considered an indispensable tool of the ruling classes from capitalist society. Especially the promoters of Radical and Critical Social Work states that the undeclared its mission is, in fact, to contribute at the maintain the capitalist state order, at the social and economic polarization, oppression, social injustice and other chronic/ structural societal anomalies.

Instead the main purpose of Critical and Radical Social Work is to move away from the traditional approaches, that were based on a medical and emotional model of the man, that places people in a passive position, with the focus on the person (especially on the material and emotional needs) rather than on the society and community as a whole, on the structural and systemic level, from where, according to the theoreticians of Radical and Critical Social Work, derived the chronic social and human problems. Thus, through its constitutional nature Critical Social Work is established also as a response and critical attitude, even revolutionary, against traditional/ conventional social work, promoting values, categories or practices such as: social change and community empowerment, structural social work, social justice, anti-oppression policies, radical changes.

If Traditional Social Work focuses the concern on the person welfare, here and now, in Critical Social Work the emphasis falls on the determination of some political structural transformations and changes so that the welfare to be derived from the optimal socio-economic structure/ constitution and the social justice, ontological-functional established. To this end, the authorities, services, institu-tions and practitioners being, thus, interested to a deserved and enduring welfare, with respect for the fundamental values of human dignity and rights, obtained both through social progress and change as well as through empowerment (especially the communities).

Between the two ideologies and policies of social work is situated, after our opinion, the humanistic orientation, Humanistic Social Work. The process of establishment, of this relatively new way in social work, is closely related to the offensive of humanistic thought in ideology, science and social practices, in psychology and psychotherapy, in microsociology. All in the context designed by postmodernism/ post-postmodernism in social theory and practice areas. Humanistic Social Work embrace social ideas, concepts and methods from the two established stances, but also brings many new, emergent, elements, according to the new social, human, economic, cultural realities and societal trends, and the new achievements in politics, science and practice. In this way, in addition, it can be stated that humanistic social work could become one of the most important doctrinal/ methodological solution for many social and community problems in the present and in the future.

The necessity of a humanistic approach on the activities of authorities, services and institutions of social work, with emphasis on the theories and practices of empowerment and change, become evident especially after the fall of communism in Central and Eastern European countries, which collapsed several aspirations to achieving a society without inequality and oppression and with the impact of the economic crisis, which reduced many resources with whom to be helped the vulnerable peoples, individuals and social groups in need or difficulty, through the redistribution arrangements and social control, shocking seriously the welfare state.

The humanistic theory and methodology comes, in this context with solutions which combines elements from the two orientation, in crisis, from the traditional social work the interest for the person as human being, and from critical social work the interest for change and empowerment, the person and community, but propose yet a proper theoretical, doctrinal and methodological system, including upon the mission and activity of the authorities, services and institutions.

In order to assert and promote a humanistic perspective on the politics, activity and practice of the authorities, services and institutions in social work the HUMANISTIC SOCIAL WORK Project operates with the phrase *humanistic social work "system"*, through which is placed in second plan the economic and functionalist values of the activity of authorities and services, and place in the first plan, as ethical-axiological and ideological foundation, the value-concept of worthy human being, autonomous and happy, obtained by personal and community development and empowering.

So, the concept *humanistic social work "system"* links the personal welfare to community welfare, and promote the development of both through human and cultural empowerment/ development. The concept involves also a humanistic perspective on community and society as a whole, and operate with the value-concept *humane community* and *humane society*. It is both an ideal, a system of values, a model, but also an objective of the authorities and services' activities.

As a community is more developed in human, cultural, moral, economic terms, the more its members are safe from vulnerabilities and the risk to getting in trouble. The humanistic social work axiology promotes, so, the importance of the socio-human and cultural factors in groups and society, in personal and community welfare, placing in second plan the technological, economical, material factors. In this end, and the activities of the services and institutions are focused on the socio-human and cultural changes and empowerment, both at the individual and group (family, communities, organizations, institutions) level, putting a great emphasis on maintaining a high level of harmony and socio-human functionality in communities, and restoration the breakdowned socio-human relationships and cohesion/ compathy, especially in families and care institutions.

In the care institutions, for example, very important are the quality and style of the management. The manager. also the worker, from a residential/ care institution, in the view of humanistic social work values, is a "man with a big heart". The humane/ soulful qualities, the positive, compathetic, visionary personality gives to manager's behavior flexibility, adaptability, sociability, communication, agreeability, tolerance, focuses it on the *human* goals of the care institution, help to prevent and resolve serious conflicts at all levels – intrapersonal, interpersonal, of group or institutional, enhances the complacency degree of customers and staff, of satisfaction (happiness), enhances the positive feeling of belonging to the organization.

Thus, in conclusion, in humanistic social work system the authorities, services, institutions and professionals are interested of material wealth, food, housing, material comfort but especially of human and spiritual/ cultural wellbeing of the community and person, of the dignity and condition of human being of the client. The quality of human relationships, cultural quality of the community where lives the client, the quality of socio-moral climate are important factors that helps him to overcome the difficult situation, to reintegrate into the community and to be fulfilled as person.

# 7.

## ESTABLISHING AND PROMOTING THE SPECIFIC AND CORE MISSION, VALUES, OBJECTIVES AND PRINCIPLES OF THE HUMANISTIC SOCIAL WORK PRACTICE

In this perspective the mission of humanistic social work practice would be to promote a compathetic attitude in the practitioner-client relationship, by creating a socio-human environment based on empathy, love and humanity, by humanizing the community, by changing the customers and communities through empowerment, personal/ community development and responsibility, starting from the person/ community right to happiness and well-being, but and from their right to dignity and self-determination.

One of the most important mission of the humanistic social work practice is the interventions in the personal and social crises, dramatic or at limit situations. The professionals from social work services are faced and with social and human problems caused by political or economic crises, social, natural or health disasters, blows, with great economical, psychological or medical impact. Some of these cannot be overcome because of the force of impact, damaging, irreparably, destinies, lives, careers, families, communities.

The affected people and communities experiences individual or collective dramas, impossible to describe, which the workers from social services must to intuit the human dimension, to represent them at the true intensity and meaning, to be helpful and to intervene through the humanistic social work methods, to improve the situations, relief of suffering and mitigate the effects, especially on children.

Decrease the pain of unhappy customer, growth the spiritual well-being, personal development and gaining autonomy through empowerment, personal/ social/ moral/ spiritual development and social-human integration are among the most important tasks of the humanistic practitioner. In the complex and unitary methodological context the humanistic practitioner will focus especially on the spiritual, psychological and socio-human sphere of the client's personality.

The goal is and the ontological harmonization of internal and external relationships within the group/ community, with effects on the development of the personality's ontological consistency of the person/ client and diminishing the risk to entry in risk or difficult situation.

So, one of the most important role of the humanistic social worker is to enable the client, a person or community, to become capable of coping with the crisis situations and difficult situations which can appears any time. This must to promote, also, the social justice, personal development of the customers, the complexity of human being, methodological flexibility, valorization of the client's creativity, development of the Self and the capitalization of spiritual potential of the human personality. The humanistic social worker have also a consistent role of educator, trainer, which involves mainly giving information and developing skills to clients, but first, must be a good educator, must to be himself knowledgeable and a good communicator.

Humanistic social work, which, up to a point, is identical with the social work/welfare as a whole, highlights, according to the most important guidelines of humanistic thought, respectively ontological-spiritual, positive-psychological, and ethical-philosophical, the following fundamental types of values, concepts and objectives in practice: promoting the person/client as a concrete and complex human being, the happiness and its fundamental interests, feelings and values; promoting the spiritual well-being and development of the person, and the cultural and moral well-being and development of the community; promoting the human development, empowerment and self-determination of the person/client and community; promoting the human dignity, social justice, equality, solidarity, compathy.

The main resources for solving the problems in humanistic social work practice are the human micro-community (compathy) and the actors' personality (empathy) involved in the process of intervention and social/ human reintegration. The client and the professional form an human-ontological unity in the process of rehabilitation, empowerment and social/ human integration. According to Malcolm Payne (2011) at the base of the humanistic social work practice should stay the following objectives and principles: accountability, psychological efficacy and social agency, achieving personal and social equality, flexibility in human life and professional practice, complexity in human life and professional practice, achieving caring and creativity in practice, developing self and spirituality in practice, developing security and resilience in practice.

# 8.

# ESTABLISHING AND PROMOTING
# THE HUMANISTIC SOCIAL WORK
# METHODOLOGY AND METHODS IN PRACTICE

Essentially, the specific methodology of humanistic social work, of the HUMANISTIC SOCIAL WORK Project, puts in the forefront the casework's concepts, values, principles and practices. Of course, into the humanistic social work practice frameworks we'll talk about humanistic casework.

Through the humanistic casework methodology the professionals, in humanistic social work system, attempt, mostly, to help people who have psychological-spiritual and socio-humane problems, to help people who have difficulties in coping with the problems of daily living.

Of course, it is one of the direct methods used by professionals, services and authorities in humanistic social practice, in assessment, intervention and monitoring, which uses the case-by-case approach for dealing, especially, with individuals or families as regards their psychological-spiritual and socio-humane problems, involving here in particular the problems of adaptation / integration, and those that cause great sufferings.

Besides, or the in the context of using the humanistic casework, the methods adopted/ adapted from the humanistic psychology/ psychothcrapy, the appreciative methods and the balance method are among the most important methods, methodological resources of the humanistic social work practice.

The methods adopted/ adapted from the humanistic psychotherapy brings in humanistic social work practice the principle of rehabilitation (social/ human integration) by focusing on the client's needs and feelings, through human and spiritual development, concentrating the intervention on the resource and strengths and not on the problem. The core idea of the client-centered therapy is that, in therapeutic process, to take the clients' accounts seriously, because they are the basis for helping, by finding their inner resources in his personality and concrete human relationships. Idea very useful also in social work, more so in humanistic social work. Gestalt psychotherapy emphases the importance, for the client, being aware of the *here* and *now* and accepting responsibility for his situation, while positive psychotherapy is based on the beliefs that all people are fundamentally good and they have the personal-constitutional capacity to be happy.

Appreciative methods promotes, as objective, the solving of social/ human problems through the appreciation, knowledge and increasing the optimistic, positive clients' expectations related to his personal evolution and the results of the intervention/ support activity.

Balance Method is a humanistic method both of evaluation and intervention/ support/ care, which operates with the following onto-balances: the balance of socio-affective onto-systems; the balance of socio-cognitive onto-systems; the balance of relationships and role-status onto-systems; the balance of attitudinal, cultural and spiritual onto-systems, etc.

The HUMANISTIC SOCIAL WORK Project, despite the appearances, attach great importance to the scientific method, to research and the evidence-based practice. It uses the evidence-based methods and practices to understand and address scientifically the human relationships and behavior, human growth and the social issues, to respond responsibly to the enormous complexity of the human personality and community.

# 9.

# ESTABLISHING AND PROMOTING
# AN *EXPRESS* HUMANISTIC
# CODE OF ETHICS IN PRACTICE

The *humanistic* social work code of practice puts in the center of attention the value of *human dignity*. In this sense, the representation and approach, in theory, axiology and practice, of the client as *human being* involves a greater responsibility to take in consideration the needs for happiness and a good live, in parallel with the concern for the customer's empowerment and autonomy.

So, in humanistic social work "system" the activity is based on the value, dignity and uniqueness of each and every person, respect for their rights at liberty, equality, and happiness. One of the main task of the professionals is to improve and empower individuals, families, groups and communities, to encourages their autonomy, their subjectivity, their capacity to assume responsibility.

In accordance also with the provisions of the *Code of Ethics of the National Association of Social Workers*, from United States, the humanistic practitioner appreciate and works for empowering the personality of every client, he respects any client who has a query, a need or a problem, as a person who is unique and distinct from others in a similar situation, and takes into account the concrete socio-human circumstances where he live.

No one, in the humanistic social work "system", must apply any form of discrimination in the execution of his profession, whether in terms of age, gender, marital status, ethnicity, nationality, religion, social status, political ideology, mental or physical disability or any other difference that characterizes any one person.

The humanistic worker use all their professional qualities and skills to encourage clients to be self-determined, self-sufficient and pro-active participants in course of action undertaken to assist them, and to foster a relationship based on mutual trust. To this end he takes into account the particular client's cultural characteristics.

The humanistic social worker must behave in a manner consonant with the decorum and dignity of the profession. He may not, in any circumstances, abuse his professional status. This must ensure that his professional competence and skills are always up to date so that he can use them to assist clients until such time that any problems have been resolved or for as long as he is legally required to do so.

The humanistic social worker must respect the right of the clients to privacy and confidentiality within any limits imposed by prevailing laws. He has the obligation to treat all information and material obtained about them as confidential and he must obtain informed consent to use it. Is required to exercise professional secrecy regarding what he knows as a result of his work, whether he is employed by a public or private body or whether he is self-employed.

In humanistic social work "system" every professional has an active role in the promotion, development and advancement of all integrated social policies aimed at fostering social and civic advancement, emancipation and responsibility within the community, and in any programs designed to improve the quality of life.

Also, he must deal with his colleagues, and any other professionals, with whom he is working, in a manner that is honest, polite, loyal and in a spirit of collaboration. His activity, conduct and decision is based on the scientific elements of the profession at all levels and in all their various forms, along with the ethical and moral ideals it embodies. Furthermore, he must act in a committed manner and under professional supervision and research.

# 10.

## PROMOTING AND DEVELOPING A HUMANISTIC PERSPECTIVE ON THE PRACTITIONER'S PERSONALITY, BEHAVIOR AND ACTIVITY; HIGHLIGHTING THE IMPORTANCE OF THE HUMANE AND SPIRITUAL QUALITIES OF THE PROFESSIONAL AS CORE RESOURCE OF PRACTICE

Promoting the importance of a humanistic approach on the practitioner's personality, behavior and activity,  the importance of the humane and spiritual qualities of the professional as core resource of practice in one of the most important purpose of the HUMANISTIC SOCIAL WORK Project.

Because between the professional's personality and the client's personality it establishes a high degree of congruence, (empathetic, human, spiritual) the cultivation of spiritual and human values of the professional's personality, as well as the development of a consistent specific literature related to the professional's conduct and activity is an important theoretical concern, the topic approached with predilection, in the humanistic social work theory and methodology framework.

Through qualities and conducts as kindness, altruism and empathy, helpfulness, through creativity, aesthetic sensibility, authentic faith, concern for truth, balanced personality the professionals will send and stimulate the development of spiritual features at the customers level too, factually sending to them positive energy, happiness, aesthetic, intellectual, spiritual, playful energy and qualities; thus contributing at their personal development, increasing the self-esteem, social consciousness, the capacity of initiative, social autonomy, fulfilling the true mission of the humanistic social work practice.

So, it will transmit empathy, humanism, agreeability, happiness and balance to the customers, will help their personal development, enhancing the social reintegration perspectives, knowing that the personal and social autonomy is conditioned also of the degree of personal development or happiness.

The objective of practice, focused on person/ client, would be to stimulate the development or formation of a personality structure where the spiritual formation is consistent and has high percentage in the structure and economy of the personality - the client will have an optimistic but realistic self-perception, a relatively high self-esteem, confidence, aspirations, a consistent ego. Also, this will be describe like an active, adaptive person, with functional interpersonal relationships, presence of spirit, eager for social reintegration and regain the dignity.

The professional and client's empathy is, without doubt, one of the most underused therapeutic resources in the social practices, including social work. But the humanistic social work give its a crucial role. In practice, empathy and compathy must to be represented and approached as phenomena and processes of very great complexity, depth and finesse, that involve the professional's personality and feelings, and the client's personality and feelings, that involve, in the assistential/ therapeutic/ educational process, the persons and the group/ groups, the individual and the society, the group and the society, feelings and representations, values and beliefs, feelings and ideas, the material and spiritual existence.

That is the reason why the empathetic/ compathetic capacity of the worker's personality and behavior is not an alternative, an option, but a consubstantial necessity of any profession on the social work field, particularly in the child welfare and social work, but also in the elderly and disabled. Through empathy the worker's personality becomes sensitive to the sufferings and problems of the people in need, and, at the behavioral level, acquires agreeability.

Others important personality resources and qualities of the worker in humanistic social work practice are the happiness and spirituality. There are a number of personal/ personality characteristics such as level of happiness, interior comfort, irony, relaxed attitude towards life hardships and professional difficulties, ie the soulful welfare and happiness, which are crucial qualities in social work practice, because they are the source of human/ humanitarian sensitivity, the empathy and agreeability - defining features of the professionals, especially those working directly with children.

The importance of spirituality, as quality of the professional's personality, is given by the fact that the relationship with the client is not objectual but "spiritual". The term can help us to understand more deeply, completely and complex the nature and specific of the professional-customer relationship. Beyond the primary goal of the social reintegration or economic rehabilitation, the customer expects also related services such as tolerance, understanding, humor, aesthetics sensibility, morality, creativity, spirituality. It is, so, impossible to imagine professional efficiency in the jobs that involves working with people in need and suffering, without empathy, soulful welfare and happiness, and spirituality.

In conclusion and the synthesis, we believe that the following personality's qualities, predispositions and conducts determines the efficiency of the professional in humanistic social work practice, in the activity to achieve the specific professional tasks: empathy, soulful welfare, state of happiness, spirituality, agreeability, extraversion, sociability, tolerance, openness to new ideas, epistemological and methodological flexibility, mature personality, emotional stability, self-control, detachment, etc.

On the view of the humanistic values, principles and theories the *training, recruitment* and *appraisal* of the personnel is a unitary phenomenon and follow that the worker in this field to not be some mere servants who simply deliver some "services" but a complex human beings, with a strong soul, with empathetic personality, with a deep knowledge of what is the man as being extremely complex. The social worker of the beginning of the third millennium is able to contribute effectively both to reducing the client's suffering and increase their ability to adapt and autonomous integrate in community. The formative-educational objectives are achieved mainly by promoting the humanistic values and model of the professional in social care areas through the specific literature or through the educational system, by increasing the number of humanistic courses, of humanistic psychology, pedagogy and sociology, of philosophy, culture and spirituality.

This is because the humanistic social worker, caregiver or psychologist is focused, with priority, on the soul, on the spiritual, empathetic, subjective, emotional issues of the client, on the existential bottlenecks, on group and personal dramas, on the moral and spiritual aspects of the problem. For this, the real problems are of human, emotional, spiritual nature.

The assessment of the personality traits such as *altruism, agreeability, tolerance, kindness,* etc. and not just strictly the instrumental technical professional skills and knowledge is increasingly a common practice in the recruitment and evaluation of staff in social care/ welfare system. The reason is very simple: to work with people, especially the suffering, difficulties and personal failure, calls for these qualities.

In the assessment process, therefore, are followed, in this context, personality traits such as playful spirit, cheerfulness, good general appearance, sociability, human (humanitarian) sensitivity, agreeability, vocation for working with the person in distress, balanced personality, interior comfort, irony, flexibility, extroversion, tolerance, nondiscrimination, adaptability, respect for life, happiness, idealism, confidence, emotional stability, self-control, presence of spirit, resistance to frustration, openness to new ideas and values etc.

Conversely, the following devices, disposition and personality factors limit, hinders the worker efficiency in the effort to achieve the professional duties: insensibility, unhappiness, chronic psychological distress, intolerance, depressive background, resistance at change, tendency to conserve a system of values and norms, opposition to new, conformism - obedience, lack of flexibility and suppleness of thought, dogmatism, reduced adaptability, stubbornness, misconceptions, unfounded ideas, attitudinal rigidity, resistance to information and change, to correction, inflexible attitudes to food, dress, political preference, sexual orientation, minorities, discrimination, emotional lability, immature personality, increased irritability, selfishness, lack of presence of spirit etc.

The core idea of the HUMANISTIC SOCIAL WORK Project is that the practitioner not only provide compensatory aid, or merely offers "services", it does not work only for the customers' survive, even if these are important tasks, but seeks to relieve the client suffering, and change his social condition through his agreeable presence, through its personality's altruism and optimism, through its opened mind and soul.

# PART II

# HUMANE AND SPIRITUAL QUALITIES OF THE PROFESSIONAL IN HUMANISTIC SOCIAL WORK

The
HUMANISTIC
SOCIAL WORK
Project

# INTRODUCTION

This section of the book proposes, from a postmodern and post-postmodern position, an innovative approach on the professional's qualities and conducts, with a great attention paid to the humane and psycho-spiritual qualities such as empathy and compathy, spiritual welfare and virtue, happiness and eudemonic-altruistic energy/ motivation, personal development, humane development and huma-nity.

Because, in practice, between the practitioner's personality and the client's personality is established a high psychological-ontological congruence (emotional, empathetic, humane, spiritual) the cultivation of the spiritual, humane and eudemonic-altruistic values and resources of the practitioner's personality is an important theoretical concern, the topic approached, with predilection, in the humanistic social work theory and methodology framework.

Structurally, this part of the book is composed of free chapters.

Chapter 1, *Humanistic Social Work - The Third Way in Social Work Theory and Practice*, is devoted to present the concept, doctrine and specific of humanistic social work, with emphasis on its main sources, values and theories, to circumscribe, philosophically and doctrinally, the humanistic social work as *the third way*, alongside Traditional/ Conventional Social Work and Radical/ Critical Social Work, in the contemporary social work practice and theory, with the claim to imposing even dominant in the future.

The Chapter 2, *Humane Personality And Soul – Personal-Psychological Sources of the Professional's Humane and Spiritual Qualities,* shows what might be called the psychological-ontological sources of the practitioner's humane/ spiritual qualities in humanistic social work practice, mainly the affective/ social soul, the spiritual soul (mystical, playful, aesthetic, moral, intellectual) and the humane soul, but is not negligible nor the role of the axiological-moral/prosocial sphere, the motivational-energetical sphere of the humane personality.

The humane and spiritual qualities, traits, or resources, such as empathy, virtue, spirituality, happiness, humanity, and more, are expressions of some personal constructs of a maximum complexity, generated by the existence of a mega-system that exceeds both the ontological and psychological sphere, involving the person as a whole, represented in the ancestral and socio-cultural context; dimensions projected mostly in what, in the paper, we call the *humane personality.*

Ultimately, the personality's model of the professional in humanistic social work, capable of generating qualities such as empathy, virtue, spirituality, happiness, humanity, altruism, is the humane personality that combines the global personality developed to a higher level with the personality structured so that determines effective professional conduct both in the objectives regarding the social integration and also in the ones of diminishing the client's suffering, or of happiness.

In the Chapter 3, *Humane and Spiritual Qualities of The Professional in Humanistic Social Work Practice,* effectively is reached the content of topic proposed by the book's title, approaching the aspect regarding the humane and spiritual qualities of the professional starting from the category of "humane personality of the professional", and insisting on the necessity to define it in connection with the spiritual-humanistic mode/ way of representation and approach of the customer.

In practice, in case work, in caring and education in a residential institution, the psychological-spiritual and humane qualities of the professional, respectively empathy and compathy, spiritual welfare and virtue, happiness and eudemonic-altruistic energy/ motivation, personal development, humane development and humanity, addressed in the chapter by reference to criteria of activity effectiveness and achieving the objectives, are of great importance too in the goal regarding the organizational congruence, consistency, unity and functionality. In these institutions, the empathy, for example, must have a very important role. The professional-client inter-empathy has an undeniable curative function.

In the same chapter is trying a presentation of the most important humane and spiritual qualities of the social worker, of the psychologist, of the caregiver, the manager, the supervisor, and of others social work professionals in humanistic social work/welfare "system", especially in child and family social work/welfare and in the care/ residential institutions.

# Chapter 1

# HUMANISTIC SOCIAL WORK –
# THE THIRD WAY
# IN THEORY AND PRACTICE

# 1.1. Theoretical-Doctrinal Context and Specific

## 1.1.1. Context

As philosophy and theory, humanistic social work is a conglomerate of theories, paradigms, orientations, but that have some crucial ideas as vectors:

- emphasis on personality, human relationships and micro-community, as basic resources of practice;

- the human/ person rights;

- social justice;

- a humanistic perspective on the practitioner, on his qualities and conducts in practice;

- the person/ client represented as *human* being, with sentiments, soul, personality, desires, sufferings, needs of love, needs of happiness and accomplishments;

- positive, optimistic and appreciative expectation in practice, person-centred and community-centred approach in evaluation and intervention;

- concentration on the future and not on the past.

Social work, in general, theoretically and methodologically, is based on the resources of social and human sciences, philosophy and other areas of the science and practice (Howe, (2009).

This is one of the reasons why the theory and practice of social work are so complex and full of dichotomies and doctrinal or methodological contradictions, taking, so, from these the majority theories and tools of practice, but, too, the theoretical/ doctrinal debates regarding the relationships between the structure and agency, individual and society, freedom and responsibility, matter and spirit, structure and element, individualism and solidarity, stagnation and change (through evolution vs. revolution), the issue of individual and collective rights, etc.

Practically, the theory and practice of social work comes from behind, from the past, assimilating them, usually afterwards, and adapting them to the specific purpose, mission and methods (Goroff, 1981.

Thus, these determines the specific epistemology and methodology of social work to include, harmonious or dichotomous, orientations, ways, perspectives and theories of the whole areas of the contemporary philosophy and socio-human sciences: phenomenologist, existentialist, feminist, post-modern, structuralist, behaviorist, psychoanalytic, psychosocial, cognitivist, holist, functionalist, criticist, traditionalist, radical, constructivist, humanist, etc. (Payne, 2005).

Yet, at a first glance, social work, as theory and practice, is dominated by two, relatively opposed, major ways, forces, orientations, namely Traditional or Conventional Social Work and Radical or Critical Social Work. The theoretical and doctrinal debate between the two constitutes subject of many books, articles and studies.

## 1.1.2. Traditional Social Work and Critical Social Work

### Traditional or Conventional Social Work

Is based, axiological-doctrinal and methodological, predominantly on the humanistic-traditionalist values and practices regarding the relationship between the individual welfare and the public welfare, with an important religious origin and support.

Essentially, this tradition involves that the society, community have a moral responsibility, unconditioned, toward the person in need, in suffering; situations that places it into a hypostasis under the ancestral condition of human being and, consequently, the society, community, family must intervene to normalize its social and human situation, mainly through material support and care (physical and emotional), without having in focus structural interventions. to change from the ground the systemic conditions that generate or maintain the problem.

According to many authors it is the starting point in any theoretical and ideological discussion regarding the values, mission and methods of the social work, both of chronological and axiological-methodological considerations, for the simple reason that it is the first and original form, but also because it provides the fundamental system of values and purposes of the social work/ welfare practice.

Helping and caring the peoples being in difficulty and/or suffering, human/ social solidarity, redistribution, sensibility for the other's welfare are universal values and objectives of the social work, anytime and anywhere (Parris, 2013).

Biestek (1978), defines traditional social work especially through some key values and principles such as:

- First the agency and then the structure;
- Focusing on the person's distress (physical and emotional};
- Individualization;
- Acceptance, tolerance and nondiscrimination;
- Non-judgemental attitude;
- Confidentiality and respect for client as a person.


So, Traditional Social Work is less interested in the social, economic or political context, which determines or support the social problems, or in the structural socio-political progress or change, which could lead to the elimination or reducing the problems, the focus is, so, on the needs and feelings of the individuals/ clients, considering each client as a unique person, each individual must to be treated as a unique human being and not just as a structural member of a community, group or society.

The traditional social work practice is much indebted to the civic sense of people, sense of unity and appurtenance to the human species, to the specific moral and religious practices and values from the religion or culture in which it applies (Parris, 2013).

The care theories, helping theories, social solidarity theories, and humanitarian theories, mainly, underlying the traditional or conventional social work's epistemology, methodology and practice. The practitioners meet, with preference, the roles of caregiver, counselor/ therapist, facilitator, broker and evaluator.

## Critical and/or Radical Social Work

Both Critical and/or Radical Social Work were established and affirmed as critical responses la the Traditional Social Work. Traditional Social Work, as practice and method, being accused of an attitude of condescension and contempt towards its clients, while the traditional social worker being considered an indispensable tool of the ruling classes from capitalist society (Bailey și Brake, 1975).

In this sense, the promoters of Radical and/or Critical Social Work states that the undeclared mission of the Traditional Social Work is, in fact, to contribute at the maintaining of the capitalist state order, and therefore, at the chronic social and economic polarization, at the chronic institutionalized, systematic oppression, social injustice and other chronic/ structural societal anomalies.

Regarding the theoretical-philosophical sources and support, to a large extent, the modern and scientific thought and methods, the critical and radical theories, the theories of social change and progress (hegelian, marxist, structuralist, feminist), the anti-discriminatory and anti-oppressive theories, the post-colonial and new-structural theories underlying, epistemologically and methodologically, this paradigm/ paradigms of social work/ welfare

The main purpose of the Radical and/or Critical Social Work is to move away from the traditional approaches, that were based on a medical and emotional model of the man, that places people in a passive position, with the focus on the person (especially on the material and emotional needs) rather than on the society and community as a whole, on the structural and systemic level, from where, according to the theoreticians of Radical and Critical Social Work, derived the social and human problems (Mullaly, 2006).

Thus, through its constitutional nature Radical/ Critical Social Work is established as a response and critical attitude, even revolutionary, against traditional/ conventional social work, promoting values, categories or practices such as:

- First the structure and then the agency;

- Focusing on the community and structural changes;
- Community and society empowerment;
- Social change;
- Structural and systemic social work;
- Progressive social work;
- Social justice;
- Anti-oppression policies;
- Radical reforms, etc.

If Traditional/ Conventional Social Work focuses the concern on the person welfare, here and now, in Critical/ Radical Social Work the emphasis falls on the determination of some systemic structural trans-formations and changes so that the welfare to be derived from the optimal socio-economic structure/ constitution, and from the social justice, ontological-functional established.

The practitioner being, thus, interested to a deserved and enduring welfare, with respect for the fundamental values of human dignity and rights, obtained both through social progress and change as well as through empowerment. In the current activity of the practitioner the client is encouraged to claim and acquire its legitimate and funda-mental rights, and not to be at the mercy of others, or to beg help. The practitioner meets in this case, largely, the roles of advocate, enabler, negotiator, counselor and mediator.

The major issues which aims it to approach and solve are:

1. The greatest social and human problems of the society, mainly the poverty, economic and social polarization, social exclusion, discrimination, abuse, etc;
2. The structural inequalities and the oppressed/ marginalized practices and politics;
3. Promoting a determinist-holistic representation of the causes and factors that generate and maintain the social problems;
4. Promoting s systemic-societal approach to the welfare system, operating, at the philosophical level, with the structural-functionalist paradigm in problems solving;

5. The welfare is associated with the achievement of certain fundamental societal and political changes;

6. The social workers must work collectively, helping people to deal collectively with social problems, white the capitalist injustice and oppression (Mullaly, 2002).

## 1.1.3. Humanistic Social Work - the Third Way

In the last decades another orientation, in a subtle manner, gradually, seems to impose with increasing force. It's about the humanistic orientation and the logical expression, formed and enforced fairly recent and prudent in the specific literature: *Humanistic Social Work* - syntagma, theory and methods that are in process of establishing and remains to be seen whether they will get to sit alongside Traditional/ Conventional Social Work and Critical/ Radical Social Work, alongside their theories and methods, and especially if it will impose, in a coherent way, in the current practice of the professionals and agencies.

The process is closely linked to the offensive of the humanistic psychology and psychotherapy, on the one hand, and microsociology and humanistic sociology, on the other hand. All in the context designed by the phenomenology, existentialism and postmodernism/ post-postmodernism in the social theory and practice areas (Payne, 2011).

So, the abundance of the concepts and theories, methods and techniques from humanistic psychology and psychotherapy, from humanistic sociology and microsociology justify the observation that we can be, already, in the presence of a *third way* in social work, with almost certain perspective to become dominant in the future.

The explanation is found in the fact that humanistic social work incorporates concepts and methods from the two established stances, but also brings many new elements, according to the new social, human, economic, political, cultural realities and trends, and the new achievements in science and practice.

In this way, in addition, it can be stated that humanistic social work could become one of the most important doctrinal/ methodological solution for many social and human problems at the beginning of the third millennium.

The necessity of a humanistic approach in social work, with emphasis on the theories and practices of empowerment (persons and communities) and empathy, humanity and spirituality (as means of socio-human solidarity and therapeutic relationship), became evident especially after the fall of communism in Central and Eastern European countries, which collapsed several aspirations to achieving a society without inequality and oppression and with the advent of the economic crisis, which reduced many resources with whom to be helped the vulnerable peoples, individuals and social groups in need or difficulty, through the redistribution arrangements and social control, shocking seriously the welfare state.

The two major social, political and economic events have heavily affected the ontological and ideological foundation of the critical/ radical social work (anti-communist revolutions), and of the traditional/ conventional social work (economic crisis).

Such, has been greatly affected the project of the structural societal change, the construction of a society without oppression, social injustice, inequality, discrimination and poverty, especially through socio-political progress, radical change, even revolution, promoted by the radical/ critical/ structural social work, and of helping the vulnerable groups, individuals/ people in need, in suffering, through the welfare state and social solidarity within the capitalist society, promoted by traditional/ conventional social work.

# 1.2. Humanistic Social Work - Theoretical-Methodological Sources

Humanistic social work, as the third way in contemporary social work, is a theory and axiology that generates a reaffirmation/ restatement of the fundamental/ constitutional humanistic values of social work, incorporating, in the same time, in a (relative) new coherent and unitary theory, all what penetrated in social work in the last decades, especially from humanistic psychology and psychotherapy, but also from microsociology and humanistic sociology, from human rights philosophy/ movement, etc. These being, also, among the main its theoretical sources and foundations.

In this sens, regarding the most important theoretical sources of ideas and values for humanistic social work, M. Payne makes reference, as our interpretation, at three major theoretical areas, respectively philosophy (especially phenomenology and existentialism), psychology/ psychotherapy (especially the humanistic orientation) and sociology (especially the microsociology) (Figure 1).

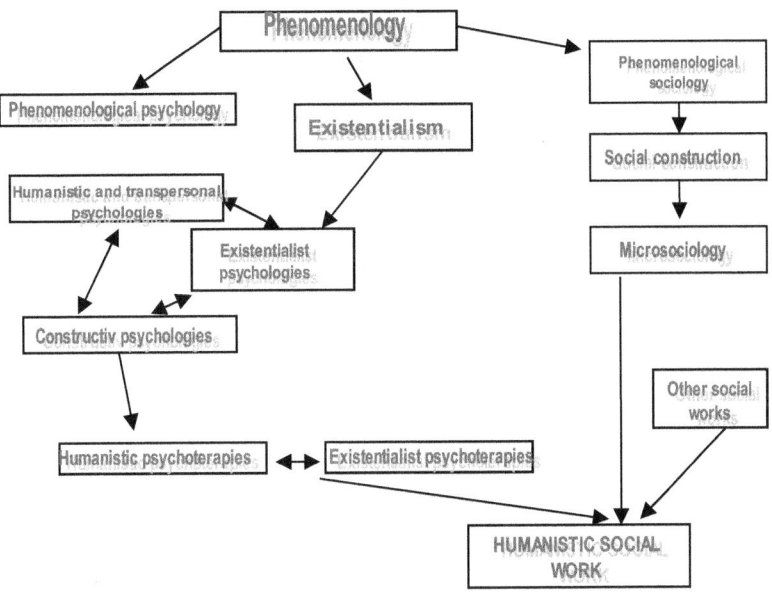

*Figure. 1.*

*Sources of ideas and values of the humanistic social work*

*(after Payne, 2011, p.9)*

In this paper we will focus on the following sources and premises of the humanistic social work theory, axiology, methodology and practice:

- Humanism, philosophy of man, the human/person rights movement/ Declaration, and

- Humanistic psychology/ psychotherapy, microsociology and humanistic sociology .

## 1.2.1. Humanism, Philosophy of Man, the Human Rights Movement

Undoubtedly, the humanism, with its phenomenological and existentialist philosophical foundations, through all its artistic, social, philosophical, scientific, ideological, political, educational dimensions, manifestations and concerns, through the multitude of themes and meanings by which it was consecrated, as system or mode of thought and action predominating the human interests, the human values and dignity, as variety of ethical theories and practices that emphasize the human fulfillment through knowledge and social development, focusing on the person/ individual/ being/ self, centering on the person's resources, the self-determination, human solidarity, humanity, human sensitivity, philanthropy, happiness, promoting the person's welfare, through the constitutional concern for researching the human being, his nature, essence, condition, through the interest for promoting of some great general human values and ideals in the evolution and development of society, through the interest for change and new, for truth, beautiful, good, represents the central foundation and essential source of the social work's theory and practice, in general, the more of the humanistic social work.

Emphasizing the importance of humanism in the theoretical, axiological and praxiological grounding of the humanistic social work, Payne highlights the aspect that:

> „Humanism brings together rational thinking, through science, with artistic creativity and imagination; one is not more important than another. The aims of that constellation of human skills are the development of thought-out value systems, innovation, and critical evaluation of ideas and actions. Democracy, human rights, and personal liberty go alongside one another in helping us achieve personal fulfillment in our lives" (Payne, 2011, p. 5).

In close connection with humanism, as movement and way of thinking and feeling, what we call philosophy of man, has an important theoretical and methodological contribution, directly or indirectly, on humanistic social work, as the third way in contemporary social work theory and practice.

In the category *philosophy of man* we include, especially, the phenomenology and existentialism, by thinkers such as Husserl, Kierkegaard, Heidegger, Sartre, Simone de Beauvoir, Maurice Merleau-Ponty, etc., with their concerns for:

- The human condition and nature;
- The person-society relationships;
- Emphasis on real, lived life;
- Interest in topics such as happiness and distress;
- The limit experiences;
- The existential crises and impasses;
- The willpower and ability to self-determination;
- Freedom and responsibility;
- The limits of personal freedom;
- The ontological congruence between person and environment;
- The concrete social existence;
- Displacement the interest from the abstract themes metaphysical, towards the existential, phenomenological themes;
- From the speculative philosophy towards the science or philosophy of the concrete, determined, existing, particular man;
- The primacy of the man as an individual, person, ego, and uniqueness in society;
- The limits of the human being, the human being fragility;
- Interest for personal growing and autonomy;
- The power of reason, of self-knowledge, of self-realization, of self-actualization.

Many of these ideas and values can be found in *The Universal Declaration of Human Rights*, which constitutes, too, important source and premise of the humanistic social work theory and axiology.

We select and enumerate below the most relevant stipulations in relation to the fundamental objectives of the humanistic social work practice.

- *Whereas recognition of the inherent dignity and of the equal and inalienable rights of all members of the human family is the foundation of freedom, justice and peace in the world*

- *All human beings are born free and equal in dignity and rights. They are endowed with reason and conscience and should act towards one another in a spirit of brotherhood*

- *Everyone has the right to life, liberty and security of person.*

- *Everyone, as a member of society, has the right to social security and is entitled to realization, through national effort and international co-operation and in accordance with the organization and resources of each State, of the economic, social and cultural rights indispensable for his dignity and the free development of his personality.*

- *Everyone has the right to a standard of living adequate for the health and well-being of himself and of his family, including food, clothing, housing and medical care and necessary social services, and the right to security in the event of unemployment, sickness, disability, widowhood, old age or other lack of livelihood in circumstances beyond his control.*

- *Motherhood and childhood are entitled to special care and assistance. All children, whether born in or out of wedlock, shall enjoy the same social protection.*

- *Everyone has duties to the community in which alone the free and full development of his personality is possible.*

- *In the exercise of his rights and freedoms, everyone shall be subject only to such limitations as are determined by law solely for the purpose of securing due recognition and respect for the rights and freedoms of others and of meeting the just requirements of morality, public order and the general welfare in a democratic society (www.un.org/en/documents/udhr/)..*

## 1.2.2. Humanistic Psychology, Microsociology, Humanistic Sociology

### Humanistic psychology/ psychotherapy

Brings in the forefront of knowledge and therapeutic action concepts and ideas such as:

- client-centred therapy (Rogers, 1951;

- personality;

- optimism;

- creativity;

- happiness;

- the individual uniqueness;

- self-determination, self-actualization (Maslow, 1993);

- focus on the particular aspects of the human existence - tolerance, love (Payne, 2011), etc.

Humanistic psychology and psychotherapy promotes the person's development in accordance with its characteristics and choices. Every healthy individual has the capacity to achieve its potential in human, social and spiritual terms, all depends of its internal activism and of the willingness for change or self-fulfillment (Plotnik and Kouyou-mdjian, 2007). These are also one of the main resources of the humanistic social work practice.

### Microsociology

It is a constitutional branch of sociology that examines with priority the laws of the micro-groups and particular socio-human contexts, focusing on the subjective/ human/ socio-human processes, on the interpersonal relationships and phenomena - empathetic, of attachment, of solidarity, of love, of conflict, cooperation, etc.

(Garfinkel, 2006) - crucial resources and categories of the humanistic social work practice.


**Humanistic sociology**

Humanistic sociology is an important theoretical source and methodological resource for humanistic social work. Related to humanistic social work, among the most important concerns of humanistic sociology are:

- the observation of how persons specifically live, love, suffer;
- what attachment relationships are established between them in relationships of kinship, friendship, enmity, interest, collegiality, power relationships'
- the resilience and coping with difficult situations;
- how they solve the problems;
- how they adapt to the changes or react to crisis or major events;
- how adjusts, interactive, their behaviors and symbolizes, mutually, the social existence (the laws, values, customs, rituals, behaviors, institutions, ideologies) (Znaniecki, 1969).


# 1.3. Humanistic Social Work - Basic Theoretical Aspects


## 1.3.1. Theory and Axiology

The specific theory of humanistic social work attempts to meets and organize, epistemological-methodological, the humanistic theory/ theories and methodology from the contemporary social work, into system, providing both a unitary theoretical and methodological framework, and a forum for debate and professional or scientific innovation.

The Theories of Development and Empowerment (person and community), Empathy Theory, Attachment Theory and Happiness Theory are, in our view, among the most important support and/or specific theories of the third way/ orientation in contemporary social work and social welfare (Stefaroi, 2012).

The humanistic theoretical paradigm, which, up to a point, is identical with the social work as a whole, highlights, according to the most important orientations of humanistic thought, the following fundamental types of ideas, values and concepts:

- Promoting the concrete and complex human being, the individuality and personal happiness, its fundamental interests, feelings and values, the spiritual well-being of the person (Payne, 2011);

- Humane personality and humane relationship like the fundamental resources of practice (Stefaroi, 2013);

- Human dignity, social justice, equality, solidarity (Humanistische Akademie, 1998);

- The exploitation of the cultural and socio-human resources from the community and social context (Krill, 1978);

- Spiritual empowerment, personal/ human development and self-determination (Payne, 2011);

- Social justice, equal opportunities, solidarity, socio-human community, human relationships (Payne, 2011, p. 4).

Empowerment is, so, one of the fundamental means, aim and value of practice in humanistic social work, achieved mainly through re-humanization, re-spiritualization and re-enlightenment of the individual and community – starting from the idea that, in the most part, the social issues and situations of difficulty have as explanation a pronounced deficit of humanism, spirituality and culture in the people's personality, or in the socio-human communities.

Malcolm Payne (2011) associate the concept/ theory of humanistic social work with the concept-value of *human being*, also with the fundamental humanistic principles in practice such as fundamental human rights, personal and spiritual development, creativity, responsibility and social justice.

So, a key concept and value of the humanistic social work theory and axiology it is *human being*. The professional-client interaction is, so, actually, an inter-human relationship between two or more beings, with personality and soul, and, the success of intervention is crucial determined by its nature and quality and not just by the economic resources or the used technology (Payne, 2011).

In conclusion, through imposing of the system-concept "humanistic social work" in the social work theory and literature it is marks the transition into a new phase, where the humanistic orientation enhances and enriches their actual presence, and makes it, more than an occasional association of terms, a strong and unitary theory, and a distinct theoretical and methodological paradigm/ way of social work and social welfare.

## *1.3.2. Core Mission and Tasks*

Starting from the stipulations regarding the mission and objectives of social work in the definition given by *The International Federation of Social Workers* (IFSW), whereupon:

> *"Social work is a practice-based profession and an academic discipline that promotes social change and development, social cohesion, and the empowerment and liberation of people. Principles of social justice, human rights, collective responsibility and respect for diversities are central to social work. Underpinned by theories of social work, social sciences, humanities and indigenous knowledge, social work engages people and structures to address life challenges and enhance wellbeing"* (http://ifsw.org/)

- we may emphasize, highlights or develop the humanistic substance of the definition regarding the social work mission and objectives, saying that the main mission and objectives of the (humanistic) social work are to **promotes socio-human change, spiritual, cultural, and human development, socio-human cohesion, spiritual and human emancipation of people, respecting the principles of social justice, human rights, responsibility and respect for diversities, underpinned by theories of social work, social sciences, humanities and indigenous knowledge, engaging people and structures to address life challenges and enhance wellbeing through** *humane and spiritual/ cultural empowerment of the person/ client and community/ family.*

In this connection, going further, the core mission and task of humanistic social work would be to promote a compathetic attitude in the practitioner-client relationship, by creating a socio-human environment based on empathy, love and humanity, by humanizing the community, by changing the customers and communities through empowerment, personal/ community development and responsibility, starting from the person/ community's right to happiness and well-being, but also from their right to dignity and self-determination.

So, one of the most important task of the humanistic social work/ worker is the interventions in the personal and social crises, dramatic or at limit situations. The professionals from social work services are faced also with social and human problems caused by political or economic crises, social, natural or health disasters, blows, with great economical, psychological or medical impact. Some of these cannot be overcome because of the force of impact, damaging, irreparably, destinies, lives, careers, families, communities.

The affected people and communities experiences individual or collective dramas, impossible to describe, which the workers from social services must to intuit the human dimension, to represent them at the true intensity and meaning, to be helpful and to intervene through the humanistic social work methods, to improve the situations, relief of suffering and mitigate the effects, especially on children (Payne, 2011).

So, decrease the pain of unhappy customer, growth the spiritual well-being, personal development and gaining autonomy through empowerment, personal/ social/ moral/ spiritual development and social-human integration are other important tasks of the humanistic practitioner (Stefaroi, 2012).

In the complex and unitary methodological context the humanistic practitioner will focus especially on the spiritual, psychological and socio-human sphere of the client's personality. The goal is also the ontological harmonization of internal and external relationships within the group/ community, with effects on the development of the personality's ontological consistency of the person/ client and diminishing the risk to entry in risk or difficult situation (Ellenhorn, 1988).

So, one of the most important task of the humanistic social worker is to enable the client, a person or community, to become capable of coping with the crisis situations and difficult situations which can appears any time. This must to promote, also, as values and objectives, the social justice, personal development of the customers, the complexity of human being, methodological flexibility, valorization of the client's creativity, development of the self and the capitalization of spiritual potential of the human personality. The humanistic social worker have also a consistent role of educator, trainer, which involves mainly giving information and developing skills to clients (Humanistische Akademie, 1998).

## 1.4. Theories and the Specific of the Theories

### 1.4.1. Theories of Development and Empowerment

The theories of personality (development) and (human) being in humanistic social work are a theoretical model and support for representing and approaching of the client as human being under development, with personality as resource for growing, with ego, will, character, sensibility and empathy, and not as a simple individuals being in a simple social, organizational interaction.

In general, the humanistic representation of the personality, approached as resource of development and empowerment, is imposed, according to our observations, by two main theories. One is the "positive-psychological" theory, another is the "ontological-spiritual" theory.

The values of these theories are part of the traditional social work theory and methodology, unfortunately, in social work practice, in many cases, they tend to be overlooked, actions and interventions are often limited to elementary care and material support. But, humanistic social work theory proposes with priority the personal, soulful, spiritual, human development as one of the fundamental objectives and tool, being therefore a inexhaustible resource available at the client and the worker level.

According to Rogers, Maslaw, Allport and other representatives of humanistic psychology and psychotherapy, Payne (2011) considers the need to achieving personal fulfillment a crucial way for social and human rehabilitation of the client. Personal development is, so, one of the key tool of rehabilitation and social adaptation of the client in humanistic social work practice.

If alongside the goal of personal and human development/ empowerment of the client is promoted also the goal of community development and empowerment certainly the number and severity of the social problems, approached, in humanistic social work, as human problems, will decrease. Community development, increasing the quality of the human relationships, the transformation of the human relationships in humane relationships are, in our opinion, very important resources, yet less used, therefore we consider these crucial categories of the humanistic social work theory. (Stefaroi, 2012, p. 166).

## 1.4.2. Empathy Theory

Empathy theory is a formative instrument used by the professionals in achieving the specific objectives, mainly in the human rehabilitation and social empowerment of the clients.

The professional-client proactive empathetic relationship is in fact a framework for transfer, a subtle lane that the professional uses, intentionally and professionally, for solve the problem (Gerdes, Segal, 2011).

Crucial is the goal of HUMAN rehabilitation and social/ compathetic integration of the client through its humanization, through spiritual development, through the development of empathetic spheres of his personality and behavior.

Empathy is a means and a purpose; the practitioner uses or creates the optimal socio-human environment for the human rehabilitation and client happiness in order to prevent the social and human problem occurred.

The practitioner uses the proactive, formative, educational and inductive valences of the empathy for the reconstruction, human-psychologically and social-compathetically, the personality and community, as step in the personal and community development and social/ human rehabilitation of the client.

## 1.4.3. Happiness Theory

The happiness theory, in humanistic social work, as theory of type psycho-social and philosophical-eudaimonical, is based on the assumption that the efficiency and the personal/ professional/ social adaptation of the person in socio-human context is closely related to the degree of happiness, satisfaction and complacency.

To this end, the psychological-spiritual well-being is a factor of energy and self-development/ autonomy, so reducing the degree of social vulnerability and the likelihood to becoming a client of the social services.

The relevance and usefulness of the happiness theory in humanistic social work is sustained by the fact that it is based on the following ideas, facts, principles:

- Every person, regardless of age, sex, nationality, race, social status, profession is entitled to a dignified life, to happiness, to personal fulfillment;

- The essential indicator of the human life quality is the internal satisfaction, subjective felt, the happiness and complacency of the person;

- The authentic happiness is a source of personal development, social/ professional efficiency and factor for the acquisition of the autonomous social reintegration capacity;

- The person is not only a simple consumer of services, of material goods, it is also a cultural, spiritual, aesthetic, playful being – this has therefore and emotional, cultural, spiritual, aesthetic, playful needs, that, for a full rehabilitation, fulfillment and happiness, must be unconditionally satisfied (Stefaroi, 2009b).

### 1.4.4. Attachment Theory

Attachment theory theorizes the importance of affection and of the attachment relationships in social relationships and coexistence, especially regarding the role of child-parent attachment relationship in the formation of o balanced and adaptive personality of the child (Bowlby, 1999).

In the child care institutions, for example, is interesting to see the role of the attachment also in the quality of the human relationships between the care professionals, between the professionals and children, as well as in the management quality and style.

# 1.5. Solidarist-Humanistic Social Work and Positive-Humanistic Social Work

As is well known, in social and human sciences, the term humanist/ humanistic/ humanism was consecrated through many meanings. We hold mainly two:

1) regarding to the human condition, the idea of ancestral human unity and solidarity; the representation of person as ontological part of a human community, mutual conditioned by the human-ontogenetic interpersonal interaction - theoretical-axiological sources of the social/ human solidarity, socio-human adaptation, and concern/ care for each other;

2) regarding to the intrinsic resources and capacities of the individual, as person, of affirmation, self-actualization, self-determination, personal achievement and development; the representation of the person as me, personality, with the attribute of will and freedom, creativity, responsibility and dignity - the sources of the personal and social change and empowerment, of the individual and the community.

The first meaning is, with predilection, exploited and stated by philosophy, religion, transpersonal psychology and anthropology, while the second by humanistic and positive psychology, pedagogy, psycho-therapy and humanistic sociology.

In agreement with the two established theoretical-axiological meanings also the humanistic orientation from social work generates two relatively distinct theories, forms of humanistic social work, i.e. the solidarist-humanistic social work and the positive-humanistic social work.

## Solidarist-humanistic social work

Supported, therefore, theoretically, methodologically and axiologically by philosophy, religion, transpersonal psychology and anthropology, the solidarist-humanistic social work is closer or even identical, to some extent, with traditional social work, prioritizing the care for comfort and welfare of the helpless person, for relieving the suffering, through various forms of help, assistance, through solidarity, altruism, compassion, attachment, empathy and compathy.

## Positive-humanistic social work

It is closer to critical social work, through the interest for changing, but not for changing the social system, the society as a whole, but through empowerment, through the exploitation and capitalization of the resources of personality and of the socio-human context with the theoretical support of the humanistic psychology, psychotherapy, pedagogy and sociology (microsociology/ humanistic sociology).

Although, strictly analytic, seems somewhat opposite, in fact, the two forms, solidarist-humanistic social work and positive-humanistic social work, are "two faces of the same coin", two sides and dimensions of the same process, subsumed to an unitary theory and practice of the humanistic social work, within the larger theoretical-methodo-logical framework of the social work field as a whole (Stefaroi, 2013).

# Chapter 2

# HUMANE PERSONALITY AND SOUL – PERSONAL-PSYCHOLOGICAL SOURCES OF THE PROFESSIONAL'S QUALITIES IN HUMANISTIC SOCIAL WORK

# 2.1. Humane personality

## 2.1.1. Personality

### The Concept of Personality

In the common language or in different social and human sciences, especially in psychology and pedagogy, the term/ concept *personality* is used primarily to refer to the ensemble of constant psychological and behavioral characteristics of an individual, highlighting, with preference, the aspects of unity of the behavior in different situations, and dominance/ consistency of certain features, especially from the temperament and character spheres (Maslow, 2011; Cottraux, 2003, p. 232).

Other acceptations highlights the importance of self/ ego as core instances in the internal economy of personality (Friedman & Schustack, 2010).

### Perspectives/ Paradigms/ Theories

Depending on the perspective to address, or other criteria, in psychology were outlined few major paradigms and theories of personality, among which we note:

- The humanistic paradigm (C. Rogers, G. Allport, R. May, A. Maslow, V. Frankl, etc.);

- The psychodynamic and analytical theory (S. Freud, C. Jung, A. Adler, etc.);

- The functionalist and behaviorist paradigm (W. James, B.-F Skinner, E. Thorndike, J. Dollard, N. Miller, etc.);

- The structuralist and typological paradigm (R. Cattell, H. Eysenck, K. Leonhard, A. Liciko, W. Sheldon, E. Kretschmer, etc.);

- The cognitive and social-cognitive theory (E. Kelly, J. Atkinson, A. Bandura, Mischel W., etc).

The humanistic representation of personality is imposed, after our observation, through two main currents/ paradigms/ theories.

## The "Humanistic-Positive" Current/ Paradigm/ Theory

The "humanistic-positive" current/ paradigm/ theory focuses, especially, on the personal development and social adaptation by using the psycho-volitional and adaptive resources of the personality. Highlights and promotes personality traits and qualities such as optimism, energy, free will, liberty, autonomy, determination, self-realization, hope, activity, consciousness, responsibility, etc.

## The Humanistic-Ontological Perspective/ Paradigm/ Theory

Highlights especially the inner-ontological content of the personality, of the self, soul, their aesthetic, playful, moral or religious resources. The humanistic-ontological perspective on the personality gives, as is natural, so, to the ontological-spiritual sphere, the primary etiological, structural and existential role.

After Rogers, the key and structural concept of the humanistic-ontological theory of personality is the self. He says that the self is an important part of the human experience, and the goal of the personality training and development of each individual is to become truly him-self by expressing and developing their potential, their own self (Rogers, 1980).

Maslow, in the book "Toward A Psychology of Being", published in 1962, reprinted in 2011, indicates an important gap in the academic/ scientific psychology theory and method, namely the relatively lack in the structure and composition of the personality, of its ontological-spiritual content, of its *being*.

In this context he envisaged that the future of psychology, implicitly of psychotherapy also of the other areas of social practice (education, social work, management, etc.) will depend, to a large extent, on the concerns and performances of redefining the human personality theory/ model/ paradigm, where to the ontological-spiritual and human dimension/ sphere will need to be given much more attention.

The theoretical model of personality that we use in this paper, developed by us, respectively humanist-ontopersonological, wherein the soul has the central role, has been used before in other ours paper appearances, respectively in the articles (titles translated from Romanian in English): "Humanistic Perspective on Customer in Social Work", nr. 1-2, 2009, "Socio-Affective Development Disorders of Institutionalized Child. From the Survival Objective towards the Happiness Objective in Social Work for Children", nr. 1-2, 2008, published in *Social Work Review* (Faculty of Sociology and Social Work - University of Bucharest), published by Polirom Publishing House, also in the book "Happiness Theory in Social Work: From Care Management to Happiness Management", Lumen Publishing House, 2009.

Aspects, elements of this theory we will present therefore in this paper, considering the soul as the central ontoformation of the humane personality, the most important source of the practitioner's humane and spiritual qualities in humanistic social work practice.

## 2.1.2. Humane Personality - Concept and Sphere

### The Concept of Humane Personality

We use, conventionally, the syntagma *humane personality* both for referring to a set of personality formations, such as soul (affective, spiritual, humane), humane ego, humane consciousness, humane character, and others - structural onto-psychological and intellectual sources of the person's humane and spiritual qualities, as well as at the humanistic orientation, quality, the overall humane valence, dimension of the global personality, meaning kindness, goodness, altruism, personality opened to the overall manhood jouissance, increased sensitivity to the other's suffering/ tragedy - itself, but also emergent resource of empowerment, wellbeing and happiness for the people from ambience; both being foundations and explanations of the professional's humane and spiritual qualities, of its humane, altruistic, prosocial behavior in humanistic social work practice.

Therefore, the complex and complete meaning of the concept *humane personality* includes the both approaches, determining superior valences (qualities/ resources) of the person/ personality/ conduct, such as spirituality, virtue, humanity, authentic happiness, etc.

## The Two Key Features of the Humane Personality

Essentially, the humane personality is revealed by two key features, namely:

1. Personality developed at a higher level, the most high, the most close to the condition of human being as autonomous cultural, rational, spiritual existence, with its characteristic attributes - morality, virtue, sociality, spirituality, personal development, adaptability and socio-human efficiency, and

2. Personality structured through the soul, ego, conscience, character, motivation, skills, etc. so that determines conducts oriented towards the wellbeing of the generalized other, towards the common good, humanity, and dominant traits such as empathy, altruism, generosity, kindness, etc.

## Basic Spheres of the Humane Personality

In our view, what is called, in the paper, humane personality, as sphere, includes at least the following sub-spheres, or can be addressed from the following perspectives:

- The psychological-ontological sphere/ perspective;
- The motivational-eudaimonical sphere/ perspective;
- The axiological-moral/prosocial sphere/ perspective;
- The aptitudinal-praxiological sphere/ perspective.

## Humane Personality and the Person/Professional's Humane and Spiritual Qualities

Starting from our topic of the book, focused on the qualities of the person in general, and of the professional in humanistic social work practice in particular, such as empathy and compathy, spiritual welfare and virtue, happiness and eudemonic-altruistic energy/

motivation, personal development, humane development and humanity we will paid particular attention especially to the psychological-ontological sphere, motivational-eudaimonical sphere, and axiological-moral/ prosocial sphere of the humane personality – all in the context of the personality as a whole.

To this end, we consider that:

- the psychological-ontological sphere of the humane personality, especially the soul, and especially the spiritual soul and humane soul, has a primordial role in determining the empathy, compathy and spiritual welfare, spirituality as personality quality;

- the motivational-eudaimonical sphere has a primordial role in determining the happiness and eudemonic-altruistic energy/ motivation of the person/ professional;

- the axiological-moral/ prosocial sphere has a primordial role in determining qualities of the person such as personal development, humane development and humanity of the person/ professional.

All in the context in which every trait, quality, resource of the personality is also an effect of system, and gains significance only in socio-behavioral context.

## 2.1.3. The Psychological-Ontological Sphere of Humane Personality

The psychological-ontological sphere of the humane personality comprises mainly two major onto-formations:

- the soul, and
- the humane ego/ self.

The two onto-formations seem to be in a relative existential opposition: the soul is an transmergent "internalization" of the other in itself, where prevails the other's jouissance, while the humane ego/ self is a subjective assimilation of the other for himself, where prevails the subject's interest, intervening here the inevitable egocentrism and the use of the humane resources, internal and external, for their own personal fulfillment and eudaimonical jouissance.

Yet, both formations, the soul and the humane ego/ self, are complementary and necessary, generating, including with the support of the formations from the motivational-eudaimonical sphere and axiological and moral/ prosocial sphere, of the humane personality as system and of the personality as a whole, the personal-psychological conditions for developing of some humane and spiritual qualities such as empathy, compathy, spirituality and virtue, necessary for the individual's coexistence and activity in socio-human communities, indispensable for the professionals which work in caring or educational activities.

So, the **Humane (moral) Ego/ Self** is, alongside spiritual soul and humane soul, one of the most important reservoir and treasure of spirituality and humanism of the persons/ professional's personality.

Because the soul (main source/ resource of the person/ professional's psychological-spiritual qualities in humanistic social work), as theme, will be discussed in an other section we will focus here on the ego/ self, with emphasis on the humane ego/ self - also, and this onto-formation being an important "piece" in the psychological-personal complex gear, generator of spiritual-humane resources necessary to professionals from the social services, in social work practice, in humanistic social work practice the more.

The formation and establishment of the humane ego contributes, leads, finally, also to:

- the establishment of the personal system of beliefs and assumed personal convictions, of the moral conducts, of the need for knowledge the human phenomenon;
- contributes, leads to the formation and establishment of the moral/ humane sentiments;
- determines the appearance of the need for social harmony, human solidarity, helpfulness.

In the internal economy and structure of the personality the humane ego meets both ontological and instrumental functions.

This introjection of the other's values enriches the own entire personality (Stets, Carter, 2011).

Essentially, the ontological-noetic content of the humane ego is supported by perceptual-attitudinal patterns like: I'm the man; 1 belong to humanity; the common good is also my good; I'm a good man; I'm selfless, generous; I am perceived as an altruistic citizen; I have dominant traits and conducts such as tolerance, compassion, humanness; I am happy through the happiness of the others; I like to help, to be useful, etc.

## 2.1.4. The Axiological-Moral/Prosocial Sphere

It includes, in our opinion, mainly

- the humane conscience, and
- the humane character.

### Humane conscience

In a very simple interpretation, but very suggestive, the humane conscience, which includes moral conscience, is an intellectual-axiological psychological universe, a superior moral instance that signals to the subject the fact that something is good or bad in the condition, existence or jouissance of the generalized other.

As against the ego, which is a formation primarily ontological, or the character, which is mainly a holistic-structural construction, the conscience, including humane conscience, is a construction predominantly intellectual-cultural and moral.

It is, therefore, the psychological-personal place where faces, debate and builds:

- the value systems of individuals;
- the conceptions towards the himself, world, people, work, society etc.;
- the place of the person's humanist ideals and beliefs (Habermas, Lenhardt, 2001).

Of course, speaking about *humane* conscience we keep in mind, also, the prosocial, humanistic, solidaristic orientation of the person's general consciousness, its humanistic global dimension, valence, oriented, by means of the systems of values, concepts, beliefs, attitudes, judgments, reflections, to the good of the other, of the generalized other, not only to the good of the significant other, dear, relative, etc., oriented to the common good, to humanity as a whole.

**Humane character**

The soul itself, as resort and constitutional source of the spiritual and humane qualities of the person/ professional, can not express in conduct than by means of some holistic and relational structures and spheres of the personality and behavior such as character, humane character.

The humane (prosocial, moral) character is a holistic personality structure through which are formed and crystallized the personal features relating to the common good and jouissance, to all people, where these personal features are stated as constant personal qualities of conduct (Miller, 2013, Gill, 2000).

Regarding the role of the humane character, its formation and establishment as structural formation of personality will lead, with the contribution of the humane conscience, to the metamorphosis of the person's humane and spiritual resources in humanistic, prosocial, altruistic attitudes and conducts.

Only by the formation and establishment of the humane character is emphasized and highlighted the humanistic valence of the global personality and conduct, is set and manifest the humane personality as a structure expressly oriented towards the generalized other's jouissance, humane personality that, by means of the system of prosocial/ humane skills, abilities and habitudes, is reflected in the person's conduct and presence as a resource of jouissance for the well-being and socio-human fulfillment of the other, for the recovery, rehabilitation or mitigation of the customer's suffering - in the case of the professional's activity into the social assistance system.

## 2.1.5. The Motivational-Energetical Sphere

When we speak about the motivational-energetical sphere or perspective of/on personality we involves concepts, ideas and syntagms as:

- Altruistic motivational system;
- Altruistic and spiritual eudaimonical system;
- Altruistic and spiritual jouissance;
- Happiness/ eudaimonical onto-formation;
- Authentic happiness;
- Spiritual and altruistic happiness;
- Altruistic and spiritual energy;
- Altruistic energy;
- Spiritual energy.

### The Altruistic and Spiritual Motivational System

It is, in our view, a superior ontogenetically construction within the general motivational system and global personality, and may be represented, succinctly, as a composition of motives, needs, trends, interests, intentions, aspirations, ideals of the person/ professional that supports the realization, expressing, disinterested, altruistic, compathetic, of certain conducts, actions, facts, activities oriented towards the fulfillment of the needs, desires, aspirations of other people, that support personal behaviors suitable to facilitate the spiritual, human, social development and welfare of the generalized other, social and psychological-eudaimonical rehabilitation of the individuals/ groups in need, suffering, in crisis (Stefaroi, 2013).

In this sense, one can speak, arbitrary of course, of two motivational-humane systems of the person/ professional oriented towards the good/ welfare of the other:

1. mobiles, needs, trends, interests, intentions, aspirations, ideals directly oriented towards the good of the other, sustaining the

altruistic attitude and behavior of aid, support, care of the people in need, which we could tell *humane motivation of help and compassion*, and

2.  the system of mobiles, needs, trends, emotions, interests, intentions, aspirations, ideals that acts indirectly, axiological and energetical, as factors of guidance, spiritualization and humanization of the person's behavior, generating the moral will and virtue, the virtuous personality, charisma, humane authority - axiological-energetical sources in the person's action and conduct, of human, personal and eudemonical development and improvement of the other, through moral and spiritual virtue, transfer and compathy, of empowerment, emancipation, fulfillment of the persons in difficulty or socio-human, moral, eudaimonic degraded.

## The Altruistic and Spiritual Jouissance

The concept *altruistic and spiritual jouissance* involves at least two major meanings:

1.  the jouissance related to higher, humane development of the personality, and

2.  the jouissance oriented towards the good/ well-being of the other.

In the first case it is mainly about of a jouissance of the spiritual soul, of the higher consciousness, moral ego and character, while, in the second case, about a jouissance mainly of the humane soul, but also of the affective (social) soul, and to other formations, higher, huma-nized instances of the personality.

In a general way, the soul, with all its areas and components, is the place and central source of the humane jouissance, therefore, if in the case of the body, senses, instinct's jouissance we talk about libido and pleasure, in the case of soul's jouissance we talk about eudaimonia and happiness, while in the case of the humane soul's eudaimonia of happiness through the other, or altruistic happiness. There is, also, an altruistic eudaimonia of the spiritual soul, and an altruistic and spiritual eudaimonia of the self/ ego.

## The Altruistic and Spiritual Happiness

Without doubt, it is hard to speak of humane personality, humane behavior, humane and spiritual qualities of the person in the conditions of a basal, elementary psychological jouissance, expressed in reactions, emotions and feelings predominantly conative, primitive, impulsive, based on the pleasure-pain hedonic-biological mechanism.

The humane personality, humane behavior, the humane, moral, spiritual qualities must have an interior psychological-eudaimonical correspondent, a jouissance to match, and the most appropriate term for this is that of *altruistic and spiritual happiness.*

Regarding the source of the altruistic and spiritual happiness one thing is clear, namely the fact that a crucial role has the jouissance of soul, of the psychological-ontological sphere of humane personality, thus representing, here, the soul as a being that feeds, develop from/ with virtue, from/ with the good/ well-being, happiness of the other, of the community, of the man in general.

At the process contributes but also what we call, in our theory, onto-personological, the happiness, or eudaimonical onto-formation. It involves the soul, but is formed, predominantly, in the onto-projective "space" of the person, gradually integrating in the personality's structure (Stefaroi, 2009b).

The role and importance of the happiness onto-formation in the process of personal formation and development, in determining personality traits such as agreeableness, optimism, charisma, sociability, altruism, empathy is very important because it improves, elevates the jouissance, the interior subjective-experiential general state, causes the person to feel fulfilled or overflow of interior well, and to externalize, contaminating, affecting for better and the other, others, perhaps more unhappy, unfulfilled, because it provides eudaimonical, psychological-spiritual energy for the general process of development, superization and humanization of personality and social behavior.

Here one can talk about what was established, as philosophical, even scientific debate, the theme of *authentic happiness.*

In our conception the authentic happiness is derived from the spiritual/ soulful and humane development, well-being and fulfillment of the person, as well as from the humane ego/ self development and fulfillment, because it is an eudaimonia of a psychological-ontological type, deeply, involving, holistically and transtemporal, the personality as whole, is permanent, is a being, an existence, and not an emotion or pleasure of moment.

Thus, the ego will not be a contingent conative, autonomic, self-sufficient ego, subject of the organic fluctuations, of impulsivity, egotistic emotions, but an universalized, spiritualized, humanized, superized ego, the personality's eudaimonia involving, so, not only the resources of pleasure and jouissance of the self but the cultural resources of virtue and moral good of the entire humanity.

Results, from here, a happiness of the person as a *human being*, a true happiness, a interior world and a psychological-spiritual, eudaimonical welfare that exceeds the personal need of internal homeostasical jouissance, the surplus, thus, pouring in outside, in behavior, in social activities, practices, energy that reaches, so, also at the other, possible in difficulty, through the altruistic, humane behavior of the subject, through charisma, agreeableness, transfer of spirituality, virtue and happiness.

## The Altruistic and Spiritual Energy

Without a doubt, the main energetic source of person's humane beha-vior, and one of the crucial resorts of the humane and spiritual qualities is the soul: affective (social) soul, spiritual soul and humane soul.

The explanation is simple: the soul is a being, an existence, an ontos, a spiritual/ transpersonal "organism" with a, relatively, own internal genesis and dynamics, as well as a producer and accumulator of humane and spiritual energy.

The altruistic motivation, jouissance, attitude, conscience and beha-vior are, energetically, supported by the soul because the soul was constituted through the transmergent internalization of the other, and the gained energy is actually a resource for the other's jouissance. The organization of the soul's energetic jouissance follows, largely, the other's organization and existence jouissance.

In this sense it can states that:

- The social-eudaimonical interaction with the other real, close, dear person, with the reference group, with the nearest physical environment, leads to the formation of the energetical jouissance of affective soul;

- The cultural-eudaimonical interaction with the spiritual/ cultural world leads to the formation of the energetical jouissance of spiritual soul;

- The moral-eudaimonical interaction with the generalized, symbolic other, value-person, through the mental facilities of generalization, idealization, symbolization and valorization leads to the formation of the energetical jouissance of the humane soul.

In the forming process of the motivational-energetic system of soul and personality are involved the instincts, emotions, cognition, will, skills, structures, automatisms. The formation, with their involvement, of some mechanisms, automatisms, montages, complexes, patterns of functioning of the jouissance and motivational system oriented towards the good and spiritual empowerment of the other represents actually the stage where it can speak about altruistic and spiritual energy, as constitutional resource and component of the motivational-energetic system of global personality.

The altruistic and spiritual motivational-energetic system is a superior ontogenetically construction within the general motivational system and overall personality, and it can be represented, succinctly, as a set of energies associated of some motives, needs, trends, interests, intentions, aspirations, ideals of the person that support the achievement, expression, disinterestedly, altruistic, compathetic of some behaviors, actions, facts, activities oriented towards the fulfillment of needs, desires, aspirations of the other people, communities, etc. (Bergson, 2007).

In this case we can speak of energy of the humane personality - resort, factor, indispensable resource of the altruistic behavior of the person/ professional, energy that not emerge from a circumstantial decision of the individual to contribute to the present welfare or change the person in difficulty, but an energy, resource existing permanently at the whole being level, corresponding of an eudaimonical-spiritual welfare and motivational structure of the personality, constitutionally oriented towards the good/ well-being of the other, towards the common good/ welfare.

## 2.2. Soul

### 2.2.1. Concept and Sphere

The meaning of the concept *soul* that we use in this paper is not identical, in sense and scope, nor with the one consecrated in ancient philosophy, especially by Aristotle (Aristotle, Robinson, 1999), and frequently used also today, of psychic, nor with the one religious, mystical, of spirit/ ghost/ sacred, even if it do not exclude them, but refers to a *set of psychological-ontological formations, ontogenetically formed and established, in the context of some objective premises and factors such as the human body, sensations, feelings, needs, subjective and social experiences, the natural and cultural context, and, especially, of some factors such as the characteristics of the nearest persons, the continuity and consistency of the social interactions, of the particular human relationships of attachment, communication, coexistence, love.*

In other words, the main source of formation of the person's soul is THE MAN/ HUMAN, with all the cultural-historical and natural systems that involves it.

Therefore, in our view, the soul is not something metaphysical, though, probably, has and such dimensions or interferences, but a very deep and complex spiritual-objective entity/ instance/ formation of the individual human being, alongside the body, personality, self/ ego, conscience, character or intellect, representing, in this context, what one might call *the place or source of feelings, of social and spiritual emotions, particularly human* (Stefaroi, 2009b).

Depending on their nature, location or source one can speak of sub-spheres such as *affective (social) soul, spiritual soul, humane soul*, etc.

Each of these soul's spheres having specific functions/ roles in determining the person's psyco-spiritual and humane qualities:

- affective (social) soul determining the attachment, social sensitivity and interpersonal/ contingent empathy;
- spiritual soul determining the spiritual richness and virtue, and

- the humane soul determining empathy/ compathy and humanity/ humanness.

Of course, all in the global context of the personality development and functioning, especially of humane personality.

The soul, as sphere, content, cumulates/ unites / synthesizes, psychological-ontologically, the subjective-sensorial experiences with those intellectual and socio-affective, generating superior miraculous unique emergent psychical-spiritual phenomena as well passion, love, faith, altruism, empathy, happiness, virtue - characteristic only of the human being.

All of these must to have a place in the sphere of personality, from where to come, to originate, to be produced by something, and that something can only be, thus, primarily, the soul, the human soul.

Thus, by forming the soul each person assimilates, internalizes, transmergent and experiential-subjective, potentially, the whole human, personal/ psychological, social, cultural experience of humanity (community), the ancestral matrix of human being, of the generalized other, acquiring, just so, the supreme quality of MAN, HUMAN, the psychological-ontological belonging to the HUMAN community, with the well known existential characteristics that it differentiate by the other modes of existence, facilitating, indirectly, mediated, also, the access to the experience (pain, happiness, etc.) of the other, concrete or generalized, generating inexhaustible psychological resources for social adaptation and helping others through the qualities they imprint to personality and behavior as well empathy, spirituality, virtue, happiness and eudaimonic-altruistic energy/ motivation, humanity, agreeableness, optimism, enthusiasm, sociability, altruism, etc. (Stefaroi, 2013).

## 2.2.2. Sources/Factors of the Soul Formation and Beingness

Even if in the child rearing are important the material conditions, the HUMAN conditions are, in fact, those that contribute crucially to the formation of the soul, of a harmonious personality, fulfilled and, socio-human, effective (Cusick, 2011, Moore, 1994)).

Each of the three major areas of the soul, affective (social), spiritual, and humane, is the product of the interaction of the subject with specific factors, even if cannot be traced strict boundaries between them. The contingent social-personal and socio-affective factors are crucial for the formation of affective (social) soul, the cultural conditions of learning and training the spiritual abilities and sensibility are essential for the formation of spiritual soul, while the altruistic, solidaristic, humanitarian, morale climate greatly influences the formation of the humane soul.

Thus, in a purely humanistic perspective, the human-personal, the human-social factors are decisive in the formation and development of the person's soul.

The psychological-human (humane) characteristics of the individuals/ persons from the environmental onto-system, as well agreeability, soulful warmth, carefulness, empathy, spirituality, their constant presence and consistency, in human, spiritual and moral terms, the human quality of the interpersonal relationships, the community compathy, the social relationships as *humane* relationships are the constitutional determinant factors that marks, crucially, the sense of the personality development, the sense of the soul development, the adaptability, the soulful welfare, the happiness.

## 2.2.3. Soul Formation and Beingness

Regarding the soul's formation, establishment and beingness in the structure, composition of the humane personality, of human personality as a whole, alongside organism, consciousness, ego, etc, the question is if its existence is necessary, if the human personality, the person could not exist, function, inside and outside, without a soul, and thus, if the conclusion is that its existence is necessary (Moore, 1994), then why, and which is its sense, role, which is the contribution of its beingness in the beingness and functioning of the global human personality, in itself also in the environmental context ?

We believe that the soul's formation, establishment and beingness in the structure, the composition of the human personality is an objective necessity, the soul being constitutional, ancestral, genetic, and emblematic part of the being, of the human personality, mainly through its adaptive function, through the experiential-ontological internalization of the social-contextual, spiritual-cultural, and human-ancestrale environmental characteristics.

We see thus, the importance of the soul's formation and beingness is undoubted, moreover, in addition to its adaptive role, very important being too the internal functional and existential role - the soul of everyone being source of jouissance and psychological energy, of existential sense, of happiness and personal fulfillment (Stone, 1999).

The formation of the soul is conditioned/ determined mainly by two processes: the development, growth, general personal development, which imposes the automatic establishment of certain formations with integrative function, and the process of conmergent organization, summary of the multitude emotional and spiritual formations oriented towards the interest of the generalized other, to common, human values and interests.

The humanization of the soul and personality is, so, an emergent holistic integrator process more pronounced in people that, through the specific activity, should engage or work with/or for broad categories of people, such as teachers, artists, workers in social, political, cultural areas, etc.

Summarizing, the soul is formed in the general context of the constitution and functioning of the specific human organism, in the overall process of forming and developing the personality, under the influence of the environmental factors and internal action of the principles/ laws of emergence, imergence, transmergence, telegence, conmergence, etc.

According to these the soul's "sphere" is a distemporalized "space", partially released by the actions of the, so-called, objective (physical) laws, the physical, chemical, biological elements involved can be easily translated, noetic, sympathetic and spiritual, and vice-versa, the possibilities and combinations becoming, practically, unlimited.

In the gradual process of forming the soul passes, in our opinion, up to the constituting, through the following stages: of contact, of acquisition/ accumulation and of structuring. After the constituting follows the instituting in the constitution of the personality, and, finally, follows his endemization/ ontification, i.e. the definitive enrollment in the psychological-ontological constitution of the person/ personality (Stefaroi, 2009b, p. 14).

The soul formation process is not automatically, simple and linear, through the mere presence of the body in society and culture. The biological, sensorial, cognitive, affective experiences, the successes, failures and traumas marks significantly the structure, organization, architecture/ composition and orientation (hedonic, emotional, social, intellectual, spiritual, religious) of the soul.

In this respect, the strong, deep, altruistic, humane personality is described also in the context of a consistent and structurally balanced soul - this becoming a fundamental source of spiritual, moral, humane energy for the person, also for the ontogenetic process of developing the personality as a whole.

Paradoxically maybe, the process of construction of the soul has not, as "pivot", the self, the subject, how we are tempted to say, but the other. This, is not necessarily an other-person but an other perceived as all out of the intrinsic order of the endemic subject.

The other can be, however, also the self and ideal ego, desirable ego, the body, the social ego, the social representations of the ourselves, but perceived as an other, through the cognitive capacity and process of objectualization. Process which lead also at the formation of the ego, especially the social ego. The soul, itself, being, in this respect, an alter-ego into own personality/ being.

In this interpretation the most important other is the ego, but follows the people who are imposed in the subject's experiences by presence and importance (they provide food, security, prestige, self-esteem, love etc.). To this end, the formation of the soul comply the structure and existence of the other.

The interaction with the other real person, dear, with the nearest persons, significant group, with the near physical environment leads to the formation of the affective soul (social), and to the personal system of attachments. Reflects the personal contingent interaction, and appurtenance of the person to the group or to the particular social context.

The interaction with the world of spirit, culture, education, art, etc., leads, by the mental capacity of idealization, projectivity and symbolization, to the formation of the spiritual soul, to virtue and spirituality as personal qualities.

The interaction with the symbolic, universal, generalized, concept other, with the "status" other, by mental facilities of the generalization, idealization, projectivity and symbolization, abstractization leads to the formation of the humane soul and to the empathy, empathetic capacity of the person. Reflects the abstract interaction and affiliation of the person to society, humanity, and his human condition and nature.

Spiritual soul and humane soul, are, therefore, the products of the personality enlightenment and of the projection capacity of the subject. In combination determines personal qualities such as kindness and humanity, human solidarity, morality, faith, aesthetic sensitivity, and humane sensitivity. Reflects the cultural, moral, spiritual, creative and ancestral quality of the individual (Stone, 1999).

The concrete process of the soul's formation is prefigured by the formation of some occasional affective, spiritual, humane micro-formations, centred, mainly, on determined "objects". Once established, they operates as relatively autonomous formations, but they are conditioned by determined relationships. Persist as long as these objects (persons, value, ideas, models) will be imposed through the presence or importance for the subject.

So, the other person, thing, habitat, situation, value, community, ideas is not regardless for the subject. Other (environment) is means of existence and vital, material and spiritual, resources, source of good, welfare, satisfaction, security, fulfillment and happiness, or, on the contrary, is hostile, aggressive, a source of stress and negative emotions. In many cases it may be also irrespective, insignificant, without influence on the formation and beingness of the soul

Some of them, especially people, concrete human being, gain a crucial existential meaning, as the mother, or, where appropriate, other person from the person's genuine micro-environment. These individuals act as socio-human/ personal "pivot" in the process of building the soul.

Yet, not the simple objectual presence of these causes the formation of the soul. The main sources of the internal onto-personal formation, of formation/ beingness of the soul are the feelings and subjective experiences in relation with the humans.

The soul, thus established as an autonomous onto-formation, tends to became a being in itself, ontological core, the person's being. Primarily through the internalization of the representations and of the empathized enjoyment of the other. The other becoming a constitutional part of the person's existence, beingness, and, inevitably, the other is assimilated and internalized by the subject's activism and her internal enjoyment.

Of course, the three spheres or levels of the soul forms, after the establishment, a bio-psycho-ontological unit, and we do not make mistakes if we consider the soul as a fundamental existential entity of the person, her ontological-spiritual nature, even if the soul's formation and beingness are dependent on the organic-psychic existence and process.

Once being established, the soul works like all the other formations, but will need of affective, spiritual and humane experiences, feelings, sentiments.

The imposing of the soul as an autonomous ontological-psychological formation and personality structure is an important step because involves the installation in the ontological-psychological system of the individual, increasing the autonomy of the onto-formation. At this level begins the process of accentuated release from references, the process of accelerated autonomisation, of acquiring an higher functional autonomy.

The person begins to become receptive to the values and critical in relation to the behaviors and attitudes of the other/close people. The soul begins to contribute essentially, hence, to the formation also of the other formations, integrative, like ego, character, an personality as a whole.

The transition to the phase where prevails the other's purposes is achieved at this stage too, is the moment where the other is represented as a desirous subject and less as desirable object. The other as desirous subject, with needs, concerns, goals is anchored deeply into the ontological structure of the person.

They can controls, by mechanisms and unconscious strategies, the personality and even the consciousness. The person accepts this situation, not necessarily intentionally or knowingly, because the other provides content for the inner life, feelings and even emotional security.

Each person is also an experiential amount of persons and entities. Only through communication, mind, language, through community coexistence, and by the unifying contribution of the personality as a whole, is defined, more or less, as a unified entity. The unification is, so, made by means of the intelligence, consciousness, ego and personality, but how these no pass, usually, the state of constituting remains to conclude that the common note of the internal persons's individual existence is mainly determined by the emotional interaction between the subject and the other, despite the established labels such as "Man is a rational being."

From the soul's perspective is essential so the presence, security and happiness of the dear, closer other. Is not a totally disinterested altruism. Person defined as a virtually assimilation/ internalization of the other enjoyment is enriched itself, because without the other it lose the opportunity to be enjoyed and humanized. At the birth, "the being", the enjoyment is in the other, the body itself is not enough for personalization/ humanization. This is the way whereby the humans access to social experience, culture, history, assimilating the all community experience, by contact with each other, with the environment, with values.

The process determines the capacity of attachment, empathy, altruism, inner well-being, social adjustment. It is extremely complex because it is made on many levels - physical, cognitive, emotional, volitional, axiological, spiritual, behavioral etc. (Cusick, (2011).

After the long, complex, deep and multidimensional process of formation, with the phases of contact, acquisition/ accumulation and structuring, after the constituting and incorporation of the soul in the constitutional structure and content of the individual's personality follows his long beingness and functioning as relatively autonomous onto-formation; processes which take place in the context of the contingent and unforeseeable social-personal, socio-affective, cultural, spiritual, socio-moral conditions and factors where the person lives, being yet established very close links, congruences, interactions, inter-determinations, compathies between the soul and the environmental system, especially with the nearest persons, with their souls; their beingness and functioning being made in inter-connection, inter-determination, mutual influence and compathetic congruence.

Even if the beingnesss and functioning of soul is not something meta-physical, probably, has also such dimensions and processes.

Depending on their nature, location or source one can speak of *affective (social) processes*, *spiritual processes*, *humane processes*, etc.

Each of these having specific functions/ roles in determining and sustaining the person's psyco-spiritual and humane qualities:

- the affective (social) processes determining and sustaining the attachment, social sensitivity and interpersonal/ contingent empathy:

- the spiritual processes determining and sustaining the spiritual richness and virtue:

- the humane processes determining and sustaining the empathy/ compathy and humanity/ humanness.


A crucial issue regarding the soul's beingness and functioning, is, what we call, the soul's needs/ motivation, jouissance and energy, as core sources for the person's qualities such as enthusiasm, energy, optimism, happiness etc. To this end, when we speak about the soul's motivational-energetical sphere we involves concepts, ideas and syntagms as:

- soul's needs;

- soul's jouissance;

- soul's accomplishment;

- soul's energy;

- soul's altruism;

- soul's consistency;

- soul's spirituality;

- happiness, enthusiasm, optimism, love, attachment, empathy, selfless etc.

The soul's needs/ motivation, jouissance and energy have, also, an important role in determining the general motivational-eudaimonical system of the personality, his spiritual, altruistic, moral, prosocial orientation. In this sense, is very important the nature, orientation, the dominant dimension, the content of soul. If it is dominant a soul's jouissance that includes the other's happiness in this case we can speak of a altruistic, humane soul, and a personality and behavior oriented to the other's well-being.

Further, one can speak of two motivational-humane systems of the person's soul oriented towards the good, welfare of the other:

1. soul's mobiles, needs, trends, interests, intentions, aspirations, ideals directly oriented towards the good of the other, sustaining the altruistic attitude and behavior of aid, support, care of the people in need, and

2. the soul's system of mobiles, needs, trends, emotions, interests, intentions, aspirations, ideals that acts indirectly, axiological and energetical, as factors of guidance, spiritualization and humanization of the person's humane personality, humane behavior, generating the moral will and virtue, virtuous personality, charisma, humane authority - axiological-energical sources in the person's action and conduct, of human, personal and eudemonical development and improvement of the other, through moral and spiritual virtue, transfer and compathy, of empowerment, emancipation, fulfillment of the persons in difficulty or socio-human, moral, eudaimonic degraded.

In this second case we speak of a spiritual soul's jouisance, that determines a strong spiritual setting and orientation of the personality and behavior. It is mainly a jouissance of the spiritual soul, of the higher consciousness, moral ego and character, and, in the first case, about a jouissance mainly of the humane soul, but also of the affective (social) soul, and to other formations, higher, humanized instances of the personality.

In a general way, the soul, with all its areas and components, is the place and central source of the humane jouissance, therefore, if in the case of the body, senses, instinct's jouissance we talk about libido and pleasure, in the case of soul's jouissance we talk about eudaimonia and happiness, and, in the case of the humane soul's eudaimonia, of happiness through the other, or altruistic happiness, and, further, of an altruistic soulful energy.

The organization of the soul's energetic jouissance follows, largely, the other's organization and existence jouissance. The social-eudaimonical interaction with the other real, close, dear person, with the reference group, with the nearest physical environment, leads to the formation of the energetical jouissance of the affective soul, the cultural-eudaimonical interaction with the spiritual world leads to the formation of the energetical jouissance of the spiritual soul, and the moral-eudaimonical interaction with the generalized, simbolic other, value-person leads to the formation of the energetical jouissance of the humane soul.

The most important conclusion of this section is that, one of the crucial function/ role of the soul's jouissance, beingness and functioning it is of generator, producer of feelings and passions. These can be positive or negative. Those negative have also the role of signaling the disturbances in the other's existence, beingness or jouissance, which can be a person, value, community, etc., and determining reactions, structures, skills and behaviors to restore the normality - function absolutely necessary also of the professional's soul's jouissance, beingness and functioning in humanistic social work practice (Stefaroi, 2013).

## 2.2.4. Affective Soul, the Attachment and Socio-Affective Qualities

In an elementary interpretation the affective (social) soul may be considered the objectual (personal/social)-affective psychological-ontological sphere/ component/ dimension of the human personality.

One of the most important function/ role of the affective soul is to determine socio-affective qualities and of generator, producer of emotions, feelings and attachments related to the concrete and significant other (Bowlby, 1999). These can be positive or negative (Stone, 1999). Those negative have also the role of signaling the disturbances in the other's existence, beingness or jouissance, determining reactions, structures, skills and behaviors to restore the well-being.

So, the main source of formation of the person's affective (social) soul is the PERSON/ HUMAN, with all psychological and social aspects that involves it. The affective soul cumulates/ unites / synthesizes, psycho-logical-ontologically, the subjective experiences with those socio-personal, generating superior miraculous, unique emergent psychical phenomena, especially the attachment and love.

By forming of the affective (social) soul each person assimilates, internalizes, transmergent and experiential-subjective, the psycho-sensorial, psycho-eudaimonical, psychological, social experience of the concrete other, acquiring, just so, the psychological-ontological quality of member of a (small) community, social group, social relationship.

The process of forming of the affective (social) soul, ie the personalization/ socialization of the soul, is an emergent holistic integrator phenomenon more pronounced in people involved in socio-affective relationships, in families, small groups, being formed in the general context of the constituting and functioning of the specific human organism, in the overall process of forming and developing the personality, under the influence of the environmental factors and internal action of the principles/ laws of emergence, imergence, transmergence, telegence, conmergence, etc.

Through forming and ontification of the affective soul the other as desirable subject, with needs, concerns, goals is deeply anchored into the ontological structure of person, even in the social ego; this can controls, by mechanisms and strategies, often involuntary and unconscious, the subject's personality and behavior, even the will and conscience. The subject accepts this situation, not necessarily intentionally or knowingly, because the other provide content for the inner life, feelings and even emotional security. Each person is also an experiential „amount" of persons and existential and virtual entities.

From the perspective of affective soul is essential the presence, security and happiness of the dear, closer other. Is not a totally disinterested altruism. Person defined as a virtually assimilation of the other's jouissance is enriched itself, because without the other this lose the opportunity to be socialized and soulfully accomplished. The process determines, also, the inter-personal capacity of attachment, empathy, altruism, love, etc.

After the constituting and incorporation of the affective soul in the constitutional structure and content of the individual's personality follows his long beingness and functioning as relatively autonomous onto-formation; processes which take place in the context of the contingent and unforeseeable social-personal, socio-affective conditions and factors where the person lives, being established very close links, congruences, interactions, inter-determinations, compathies between the affective soul and the concrete environmental (social) system, especially with the nearest persons, with their souls; their beingness and functioning being made in inter-connection, inter-determination, mutual influence and compathetic congruence.

## 2.2.5. Spiritual Soul, the Virtue and Spiritual Qualities

In an elementary interpretation the spiritual soul may be considered the spiritual psychological-ontological sphere/ component/ dimension of the human personality. Through the spiritual soul, this miraculous onto-formation of the human personality, the subject accede to culture, history, practically assimilates, experiential-ontological and ontogenetical, the evolution/ universe of the human spirituality and community through the contact with the concrete cultural environment, bearer of universal meanings, with the values, the ancestral, generalized/ spiritual human experience (Wommack, 2010, Bean, 2013).

After the establishment in the personality constitution determines the spiritual sensitivity/ development, the authentic happiness, virtue and superisation of the personality and behavior; it is, so, crucial factor in the formation of human personality, including of the professional from the social assistance system. This onto-personal formation, crucial in the architecture of human personality, is formed and established as a result of the "internalization" and organization of the noetic, ego-projective or spiritual experiences/ feelings (mystical, playful, epistemic, aesthetic, moral, etc.). In this sphere will be installed, what we might call, the spiritual-projective *being* of the person.

It is constituted on the bio psychological foundation of the personality, of the affective soul, mind, and in the context of establishing of the other personal onto-formations, which chronologically succeeding them (even if the formation and establishing processes are simultaneous or interactive).

Depending on the types of feelings, on the subjective experiences involved, of the cultural characteristics of the environment, but also by many other factors, will forms:

- the mystical soul;
- the playful soul;
- the aesthetic soul;
- the gnostic soul;
- the moral soul, etc. (Stefaroi, 2009a).

**Mystical Soul**

This onto-formation is constitutes in closely related with the phobic and malsentic (depressed) formation, the hypothesis of death, with the "non-being", with the supernatural, the superior love, with the saint as model and aspiration, with the heaven, with the fantastic/transcedental happiness, with the absolute, the infinite, the God, etc. The mystic sphere, component, dimension, valence of the person/personality is not an option, is a foundation of the personal constitution, and is materialized in the setting of certain specific onto-formations (Stefaroi, 2009a, p.22).

The mystical soul is set on the opposite side of the endemic. Both poles are still *beings*, these have autonomous existences, needs and produce specific personal motivation and desires.

The persons' mystical motivation/ desires requires:

- mystical experiences;
- the need of sacred;
- trances, revelations, sublime feelings;
- asceticism, faith, love, heroism, etc.

So, the mystical soul's formations and processes are somewhat in opposition with the contingent formations and processes of the consciousness, reason and behavior. Are deep ancestral "implants" in unconscious, landmarks of the individual's beliefs and convictions, but also sources of the emotional instability, fanaticism and paranoia (in pathological view).

In some cases, the mystical soul unites, by the sacred spirit, the body, mind, the self, environment, culture and projectiv/ transmergent/ telegent capacity of the onto-personality, inevitable for the personal/ personality's genesis/ development (Bean, 2013). The focalization of these energies and processes is creative of high spirit. Its content is the higher/ sublime emotion (sentiment, passion) - profound, almost revealed, impossible of analyzed and described scientifically.

## Gnostic Soul, Playful Soul, Aesthetic Soul, Ethical Soul

The establishment of the spiritual soul generates also aesthetic, playful, gnostic, ethical needs. They are the expression of certain spiritual onto-projective formations like the gnostic soul, playful soul, esthetic soul, ethical/ moral soul, etc. The gnostic soul has many similarities and connections with the noetic onto-formation. What differentiates them is that the noetic onto-formation is an organization of ideas in itself, an itself objective world, logical, intrinsic, cognitive, self-sufficient, while the gnostic soul is subjective and emotional impregnated, and determines the higher need of the subject to search gnosis that produce satisfaction. While for the noetic onto-formation the fundamental need is for the truth, for the gnostic soul prevailing the subject's spiritual need for the knowledge itself.

Between the two poles, mystic and gnostic soul, is located playful and aesthetic soul. The playful soul is expression of the ontological-ancestral need of the person of liberty, entertainment, of irony against the limits of existence. The personality will reflected, in its own dimension, this spirit - requirement of social, cultural, moral action, but and of creativity. The environment as source of the playful soul is a different world than the real one, is set with its elements and laws, but placed in an ontological order inherently questionable. The playfulness soul illuminates and streamline the internal communication channels and with the environment, gives to the individual comfort and authentic existence, spirituality.

From the playful soul is feeds also the process of formation the aesthetic soul. In fact is very difficult to achieve a clear distinction between the two onto-formations. However, the aesthetic soul, also the ethical soul, is reported at the established historical-cultural values, imposed by society, but subjectively assimilated by the person (Doherty,1996).

It is, so, very important, beyond the social, cultural, historical matters, the ontological-individual organization as *soul* of these values. Yet, it can be said that by imposing the values, as social/ transpersonal commandment, the soul is more regularizes, leading to an higher organization in the structure of personality also in the socio-human behavior (Stefaroi, 2013).


## 2.2.6. Humane Soul, the Empathy and Humane Qualities

In an elementary interpretation the humane soul, in our view, may be considered the general human-altruistic psychological-ontological sphere/ component/ dimension of the human personality. The establishment and ontification of the humane soul may be considered the terminal stage of the complex process of formation and ontification of the soul, as essential sub-process in the overall process of formation of the humane personality, of the personality as a whole, also of the person's psychological-ontological structures, in general.

Brings together, emergent and transmergent, at a higher level, more complex, deeper and synthetic, the onto-formations from the affective (social) soul and spiritual soul levels, generating the extraordinary ability, ancestral, unique, of the person to feel, live and think as a *human being*, as an ancestral being, as an exemplar humane being, but also as a *humane* being, by their ability to resonate, empathize, compathize with the human and spiritual experience of the other persons, even if they are not part of the inner circle of acquaintances, relatives, colleagues etc.

Through the formation and establishment of the humane soul the personality as a whole is reformed and is defined by solidarist-humanistic qualities and behavioral traits such as empathy, agreea-bleness, tolerance, humanity, human sensitivity etc. - qualities related, therefore, not only to the contingent social sphere of the subject, but to all that is human, universal-human, trans-, pan-human, anywhere and anytime.The establishment of the humane soul is made, also, with the transmergent and emergent actions of some instances and spheres from the intellectual and moral levels, which, moreover, by feedback, determines their reforming, contributing together to the establishment of the character and prosocial behavior.

Thus, by the prosocial valences imprinted to personality and behavior, the humane soul becomes a crucial factor for adaptation and social integration of the person in social groups, communities, environments, other than those based mainly on attachment and knowing each other. In this respect, the problems of adaptation, communication, or of integration of the disadvantaged persons into alternative social groups can also be interpreted as a result of the underdevelopment, disorders, injuries or weaknesses of the humane soul.

The process of formation of the humane soul, as autonomous structure and instance of personality, achieves its ontogenetical target usually in the adulthood when the person becomes sensitive to the situation of the wider community, society, humanity as a whole; the humane soul having, in this sense, a crucial role in the forming of the humanistic beliefs and convictions, solidaristic, humanitarian, also a very important role in determining the character orientation, the attitudes towards themselves, towards work, people, values, society etc.

The constitution of the humane soul, as yet a distinct personal onto-formation than the affective/ social soul and spiritual soul, as an integrated and unified formation, is conditioned/ determined mainly of two processes:

1.  the general personal evolution, growth, development, which requires the automatic creation of certain morale, prosocial formations with integrative functions, and

2.  the process of organizing, synthesis of the multitude of the affective and spiritual formations oriented towards the interest of the generalized other, towards common, human values and interests.

Of course, the basic factors of the *humane* ontification of personality are the social environment based on solidarity and empathy/ compathy, the cultural education oriented to people and values, the intellectual and of valorization capacity, the need for superior development and organization of the personality, the need for security, and, not least, the ontogenetical natural tendency of decentering of the self, of overall humanization of the personality and behavior, of socio-human integration and adaptation in groups and communities more and more complex on the course of growing.

The *humanization* of the soul and personality is an emergent holistic and integrator process more pronounced in people such as teachers, social workers, artists etc., professional and volunteers involved in specific activities for broad categories of people (McLaren, 2010).

The nature of the humane soul is probably mostly psychological-spiritual, but as a system, structure and composition is a unitary bio-psycho-cultural complex, conmergent and transmergent, which means that it is much more than a summation of the humane, altruistic feelings and passions, it is a "being", an existence also in themselves in the personality sphere.

We can speak about a genesis of this sphere, about a structure, composition, organization, content, nature and so on, but the most interesting thing in view of the theme regarding the humane qualities of the professional in social work, is its prosocial, moral, compathetic, altruistic dimension, valence, capacity, quality. Nor the functioning, nor the genesis, nor the existence of the humane soul would not be possible without a strong cultural, anthropo-social, pan-human dimensioning. Therefore, the humane soul is established and operates by two complementary cardinal processes:

- oriented to himself, of humanization and universalization of the self, ego self- personality, and;

- of cultural, anthropo-social setting, oriented towards other people, to world, society, values.

This second dimension will be the key driver for formation of the humane personality, prosocial behavior and empathy/ compathy as cardinal psychological-spiritual/ humane resources, traits, qualities of the person, including of the professional in humanistic social work

In the humanistic social work practice perspective is more than obvious the need for prioritizing the development of this sphere of the professional's personality; key humane qualities and conducts in the professional's activity of evaluation and intervention with the beneficiaries, such as empathy/ compathy, agreeability, tolerance, and more, are generated, largely, by the existence and manifestation of the humane soul; of course on the background and in the context of the global spiritual development, of the overall personal, human and psychosocial development.

## 2.3. Humane Personality, Soul and the Humane and Spiritual Qualities of the Person/ Professional

The humane and spiritual qualities, traits, or resources, such as empathy, virtue, spirituality, happiness, humanity, and more, are expressions of some personal constructs of a maximum complexity, generated by the existence of a mega-system that exceeds both the ontological and psychological spheres, involving the person as a whole, represented in the ancestral and socio-cultural context - dimensions projected mostly in what, in the paper, we call *humane personality*.

Thus, the humane and spiritual qualities are not mere expressions of the emotional and spiritual development, of the affective soul, of the spiritual and humane spheres, but rather expressions of the general cultural development, of the existence of certain skills or inclinations, of the character development, or of the eudemonic-spiritual and eudaimonic-prosocial spheres, and, not least, of the development of personality as a whole, through its humane/ humanistic orientation/ dimension, as a personality developed at a higher level, closer to the condition of human being of the person, as cultural, rational, spiritual and autonomous existence with its characteristic attributes - morality, virtue sociality, spirituality, personal development, adaptability and socio-human efficiency, as well as personality structured, through the soul, ego, conscience, character, motivation, skills, etc., so that determines conducts oriented to the welfare of the other, of the generalized other, of the community, humanity, also dominant traits, qualities such as empathy, altruism, generosity, kindness, etc.

Ultimately, the model of personality of the professional in humanistic social work, capable of generating qualities such as empathy, virtue, spirituality, happiness, humanity, altruism, is the humane personality that combines the global personality developed to a higher level with the personality so structured that determines effective professional conduct both in the objectives of personal empowerment and social integration, also in the ones of diminishing the client's suffering, or of happiness.

However, in our opinion, the central role in determining the humane and spiritual qualities of the professional in humanistic social work practice it has the soul, with the three main areas, the affective (social) soul, the spiritual soul, and the humane soul. Each of these having, so, as was shown in the paper, specific functions/ roles in determining the person/ professional's spiritual and humane qualities - the affective (social) soul determining the attachment, social sensitivity and interpersonal/ contingent empathy, the spiritual soul determining the spiritual richness and virtue, and the humane soul determining empathy/ compathy and humanity/ humanness; of course, therefore, in the global context of personality, especially of humane personality.

The main explanation of the humanistic, spiritual, altruistic virtues of the soul comes from the fact that this, as sphere, content, cumulates/ unites/ synthesizes, psychological-ontologically, the subjective experiences with those intellectual and socio-affective, generating superior, miraculous, emergent behaviors, strongly oriented to the other's jouissance.

By forming in a humanistic way of the professional's soul this assimilates, internalizes, transmergent and experiential-subjective, potentially, the whole human, personal/ psychological, social, cultural experience of humanity (community), the ancestral matrix of the human being, of the generalized other, acquiring the psychological-ontological belonging to the human community, with the well known existential characteristics that it differentiate by the other modes of existence, facilitating, indirectly, mediated, also, the access to the experience (pain, happiness, etc.) of the other/ client, generating inexhaustible psychological resources for helping other people through the qualities they imprint to personality and behavior, such as empathetic and compathetic ability/ capacity, spirituality and virtue, or contributing to the potentiation/ expression of some qualities and resources such as happiness and eudemonic-altruistic energy/ motivation, humanity, agreeableness, optimism, enthusiasm, and more - indispensable qualities of the professional in social work practice, the more in humanistic social work practice.

# Chapter 3
# HUMANE AND SPIRITUAL QUALITIES OF THE PROFESSIONAL IN HUMANISTIC SOCIAL WORK PRACTICE

# 3.1. Humanistic Social Work Practice. The Role and Importance of the Humane and Spiritual Qualities of the Professional

## 3.1.1. Objectives, Values and Principles of Practice

### Core objectives of practice

Human suffering, unhappiness, personal failure, loss, dehumanization of the individual and community, emotional drama and great collective tragedies, disasters with significant human impact, personal/ community underdevelopment are among the central problems and object of intervention in humanistic social work practice. From here starts humanistic social work the demarche of establishing his specific objectives of practice (Stefaroi, 2012).

Operating into the sphere of social, *human* relationships, the main purpose of the services and professional's activity is that *to transform them in* **humane** *relationships, starting from the idea that the suffering, unhappiness, personal failure, loss, dehumanization of the individual an community have, largely, the main sources in the precariousness social and human relationships.*

The professional's personality and its psychological-spiritual qualities represents, for this purpose, the means, the essential professional resource that can facilitate the achievement of the humanistic objectives in practice, that can facilitate the changing, through which can humanize the troubled social relationships, the dehumanized, dysfunctional micro-community, the moral, psychological damaged people, in difficulty, suffering, conflict, underdevelopment.

In this way reaching so to perform the specific mission, to determine changes not at the society level, such as the critical/ radical social work, where it is the mission of the politician, nor at the body level, where it is the mission of the healthcare professional, but at the human, socio-human level, at the human relationships level, where it is its mission.

In this mission the humanistic practitioner is involved with whole its self, soul, intellect and experience, in the complex assembly of relationships, connections, conflicts, attachments, inter-empathies, compathies, feelings, passions, loves, projects, dramas of the group with problems, he detect the dysfunctions, problems, under-developments, anomalies, building the diagnostic panel by an etiology and phenomenology of existential-humanistic type, focusing, therefore, on *highlighting the dysfunctions from the human relations level,* the intervention aiming, so, to convert them, by means of its knowledge, experiences, humane personality, soul, and psychological-spiritual qualities, as curative resources, in *humane relationships.*

The change for better from the human relations level, transformed into humane relations, will generate improvements, impressive qualitative changes at the micro-community level as a whole, as well at the level of each person; *the transformative process evolving in cascade, involving humanizing sub-processes at all levels, eliminating many dysfunctions, disorders, problems, sufferings; the new created environment being defined by qualifiers such as spiritual and humane welfare, efficiency, socio-humane cohesion, harmony, solidarity, mutual aid, compathy, responsible, cooperation, humanity.*

This environment will impose, ultimately, as a curative solution for many problems and difficult situations, and only to the extent that the professionals and social services manage to lead, generate it, with their activities, measures, conducts can sustain that they operates thoroughly and efficiently, and meet their specific mission, at least in the perspective of the humanistic social work theory and axiology.

Combining thus, in its own and creative way, the resources from the person level, respectively of the humane personality, with the resources from the community level, respectively of the humane relationships, taking thus elements both from traditional social work and critical/ radical social work, humanistic social work justify their attribute as the third way also and in practice.

In this sense, when they define the objectives and humanistic mission, the professionals and the social work/ welfare services operates mainly with terms and phrases such as:

- Diminishing the customer's suffering, distress and unhappy;
- Increasing the spiritual well-being (Goldstein, 1984);

- Personal and community development, and obtaining the autonomy (Payne, 2011);

- Moral development and socio-human integration, etc.

## Core values of practice

Humanistic social work practice put at the base of the services and professionals' activity, as core value, the client representation and approach as a *human being*, with soul, with feelings, with sufferings, with spiritual and eudaimonical needs, as personality, with ego, will, freedom and internal resources for rehabilitation and regaining the autonomy, and not just as a dysfunctional element in a social system and process.

In this sense, the professional-client interaction is actually an inter-human/ humane relationship between two or more human beings, with personalities and souls, and, the success of intervention is crucial determined by its humane nature, quality and development.

Other crucial values which must stay at the basis of the services and professional's activity, would be:

- social justice (Payne, 2011);

- personal and human development of the customers:

- the complexity of the client's personality, and of the client system;

- methodological flexibility (Payne, 2011);

- evidence-based practice;

- valorization of the client's creativity, freedom and resources;

- development of the self, and the capitalization of spiritual potential;

- the priority of the client's interests, feelings and values;

- spiritual well-being and development of the client and community (Humanistische Akademie,1998);

- human development, empowerment and self-determination of the person/client and community (Stefaroi, 2012);

- equality, solidarity, compathy;

- human relationships as humane relationships;
- multiculturality (Wing Sue, 2006);
- the importance of the professional' personality, education, humane qualities, conducts, value and principles in practice (Humanistische Akademie,1998).

**Basic values of the professional in practice**:
- humanism, empathy, understanding (Payne, 2011);
- frankness, accountability, discipline;
- doing good, respect for life, loyalty, cooperation, solidarity;
- courtesy, democratic spirit, kindness, concern, caring, giving, sharing;
- incorruptibility, respect of rights, non-violence;
- self-respect, happiness, contentment;
- truth, love;
- integrity, non-discrimination, honesty;
- humanistic/ altruistic motivation (Stefaroi, 2013);
- self-knowledge, concentration, meditation, self-control, temperance;
- gentleness, respect, resourcefulness, circumspection;
- forgiveness, equanimity;
- spirituality (Humanistische Akademie, 1998).

## Core principles of practice

Accountability, achieving personal and social equality, flexibility in human life and professional practice, complexity in human life and professional practice, achieving caring and creativity, developing self and spirituality, developing security and resilience, developments in research are, according to Payne (2011), the most important principles and values of the humanistic social work practice.

The main role of the humanistic social work practice is to enable the clients to realize their potential within the therapeutic relationship and socio-human context, by enhancing the client's potential, to achieve the self-actualization in social environment, also to create just social conditions to promote general well-being, to promote human and social well-being by developing the human capacities, social justice, equality, freedom, and mutual responsibility through shared social experience (Payne, 2011, p. 31).

*Accountability principle*

According to Payne the accountability principle, in humanistic social work, involves both the social worker and agency's responsibility and the client's responsibility. The client has, the first, the responsibility for his situation and his rehabilitation, but the social worker, as agent of community and humanity, has the professional accountability for applying the most optimal and scientific procedures, based on evidences, and to fulfill the mission given by these.

So, the professional has also a personal accountability, in relation of the humanitarian mission that he has, and of the specific of profession which he has chosen. Also, procedures that allow for informed consent and advanced care planning communicate respect for clients to make their own decisions upon full disclosure of information. This allows for client responsibility to express personal power or social agency.

To this end, accountability involves working together to create a social environment that is responsive to and supportive of client change. Here professional involves helping clients exercise political power when conditions are most receptive to social change. An environment most conducive to change is partially characterized by the presence of social policies that protect basic human rights (*from* Callahan, 2012, pp. 181-184).

*Flexibility and complexity*

Both principles of the humanistic social work practice, according to Payne, suggest an almost limitless human and professional opening to a wide variety possibilities of manifestation of the customer and to the multiple therapeutic options. The *flexibility principles* guides especially the current practitioner activity; it facilitates a flexible assistential/

therapeutic relationship that consists of an improvisation that occurs between the client and professional, and is articulated through the convention of therapeutic/ assistential rapport.

The *complexity principle* concerns the way of representation to the client, the social context and the difficult situation, especially in the way of approach and assessment activity. Payne considers that the complexity principle involves a complex and multidimensional representation of the client, of the situations of difficulty and therapeutic contexts in which operate the professional. Reactions to change may not be accurately predicted given the variety of factors involved in a system. So, the author warns against oversimplification of relational patterns that may come with problem solving, and encourages fuller consideration of a variety of perspectives to better respond to the multifaceted nature of client concerns (*from* Callahan, 2012, pp. 181-184).

*Spirituality principles*

For Payne, in humanistic social work practice, the spirituality principles is one of the most important. After the author of the book "Humanistic Social Work. Core Principles in Practice" spirituality is one of unlimited resources that are available to both at the client and the professional and involves the process of making meaning out of life events. Through spirituality the intervention process can help the clients to establish a sense of congruence with self and the world, with culture, wholeness in life and happiness (Payne, 2011).

**Code of Ethics**

What would particularizes a code of ethics of the humanist social work practice in report to critical and/ or radical social work for example, which emphasizes the importance of the systems and structures generators of problems, inequality, suffering, social injustice, is the emphasis put, in the work of the services and professionals, on the exploitation of the resources of the personalities and socio-human contexts involved in the processes of assessment and intervention.

This aspect involves a huge responsibility of the services and professionals which one can not invoke the system and structures for the failure of activity, and require from them very much engagement, responsibility, ethics, knowledge, skills, and professional relationships marked themselves of more humanism.

In humanistic social work "system" every professional has an active role in the promotion, development and advancement of all integrated social policies aimed at fostering social and civic advancement, emancipation and responsibility within the community, and in any programs designed to improve the quality of life.

Also, the professional must deal with his colleagues, and any other professionals, with whom he is working, in a manner that is honest, polite, loyal and in a spirit of collaboration.

In humanistic social work practice the professional's work, conduct and decision is based on scientific elements of the profession at all levels and in all their various forms, along with the ethical and moral ideals it embodies. He must act in a committed manner and under professional supervision and research.

From the *Code of Ethics of the National Association of Social Workers,* USA, we retain some provisions that we consider to be adequate for the behavior and activities of the professionals in the humanistic social work "system" (we keep the original form taken from the website of the *National Association of Social Workers)*:

- *The mission of the social work profession is rooted in a set of core values. These core values, embraced by social workers throughout the profession's history, are the foundation of social work's unique purpose and perspective: social justice; dignity and worth of the person, importance of human relationships, integrity, competence.*

- *The primary mission of the social work profession is to enhance human well-being and help meet the basic human needs of all people, with particular attention to the needs and empowerment of people who are vulnerable, oppressed, and living in poverty. A historic and defining feature of social work is the profession's focus on individual well-being in a social context and the well-being of society. Fundamental to social work is attention to the environmental forces that create, contribute to, and address problems in living.*

- *Social workers promote social justice and social change with and on behalf of clients. "Clients" is used inclusively to refer to individuals, families, groups, organizations, and communities. Social workers are sensitive to cultural and ethnic diversity and strive to end discrimination, oppression, poverty, and other forms of social injustice. Social workers should obtain education about and seek to understand the nature of social diversity and oppression with respect to race, ethnicity, national origin, color, sex, sexual* orientation, gender identity or expression, age, marital status, political belief, religion, immigration status, and mental or physical disability.

- Social workers treat each person in a caring and respectful fashion, mindful of individual differences and cultural and ethnic diversity. Social workers promote clients' socially responsible self-determination. Social workers seek to enhance clients' capacity and opportunity to change and to address their own needs. Social workers are cognizant of their dual responsibility to clients and to the broader society. They seek to resolve conflicts between clients' interests and the broader society's interests in a socially responsible manner consistent with the values, ethical principles, and ethical standards of the profession.

- Social workers understand that relationships between and among people are an important vehicle for change. Social workers engage people as partners in the helping process. Social workers seek to strengthen relationships among people in a purposeful effort to promote, restore, maintain, and enhance the well-being of individuals, families, social groups, organizations, and communities.

- Social workers' primary responsibility is to promote the well-being of clients. In general, clients' interests are primary. However, social workers' responsibility to the larger society or specific legal obligations may on limited occasions supersede the loyalty owed clients, and clients should be so advised. (Examples include when a social worker is required by law to report that a client has abused a child or has threatened to harm self or others).

- Social workers respect and promote the right of clients to self-determination and assist clients in their efforts to identify and clarify their goals. Social workers may limit clients' right to self-determination when, in the social workers' professional judgment, clients' actions or potential actions pose a serious, foreseeable, and imminent risk to themselves or others.

- Social workers should have a knowledge base of their clients' cultures and be able to demonstrate competence in the provision of services that are sensitive to clients' cultures and to differences among people and cultural groups. (www.socialworkers. org/).

## 3.1.2. Evidence-Based Practices

Despite the appearances, the humanistic social work praxeology attach great importance to the scientific/ experimental method, to research and the evidence-based practice.

It uses the evidence-based practices and methods to understand and address, scientifically and experimentally, the human relationships and behavior, human growth, the social issues, the situations of difficulty of the clients (Roberts, Yeager, 2006).

The evidence-based practices and methods, in humanistic social work practice, propose, in the specific activity of evaluation, intervention and change, in casework, caring and therapy, etc., the focusing on the complex, phenomenological reality of the client by scientific knowledge, experimental research and methodical embedding of the previous clinical experiences.

So, in humanistic social work practice the practitioners can/ must embody flexible, contextual, but also knowledge-based responses to the complexities of the human personality and community, to the complexity of the situations of difficulty of the clients (Payne, 2011).

In this sense, the evidence-based practices involves, in the specific activity of the practitioner, of assessment and intervention, the focusing, both contextual/ existential and scientific, on the complex, phenomenological reality of the client (Rubin, Babbi, (2012).

The construction of the evaluative picture of system client starts, yet, with what is identified as existing, real, verifiable and sensitive (Payne, 2011: 76). Further, the practitioner's work is based on the evidence of researches and studies's conclusions on that type of case it works. This having the task to realize "modelations" of the identified difficult situations in report of the research's findings, without abdicating, but, from the fundamental values and principles of the humanistic social work related to the immense complexity of the socio-human phenomena and of the situations of difficulty in which are involved the clients (O'Hare, 2005).

### 3.1.3. Methods

**The methods adopted/ adapted from humanistic psychotherapy**

Humanistic psychotherapy is undoubtedly the main source of the humanistic social work methodology and practice. It promotes the equal relationship between therapist and client, and increases the role of the personality (ego, free will) and of the affective processes in the therapeutic relationship.

The humanistic psychotherapy's methods brings in humanistic social work practice the core principles of rehabilitation (social/ human integration) by focusing on the client's needs and feelings, through human and spiritual development, concentrating the intervention on the (human) resource and strengths and not on the problem (Payne, 2005, pp. 186-187).

*Client-centered intervention*

Through the client-centered therapy Carl Rogers ((1951) has, indirectly, the crucial merit to worked at the foundation of the modern social work theory and method through the therapeutic-humanist methods and values promoted in practice.

The core idea of the client-centered therapy, promoted by Rogers and his followers, is that, in the therapeutic process, to take the clients' accounts seriously, because they are the basis for helping, by finding their inner resources, in his personality and concrete human relationships. Idea very useful also in social work, more so in humanistic social work.

Rogers argues that the client has a strong need for positive feelings, important idea for social work practice where the majority of clients are dominated by negative feelings.

In this end the social worker can use the internal experiences of the clients as resources in the process of rehabilitation, empowerment, normalization.

*Existential psychotherapy/ intervention*

The existential psychotherapy focuses, especially, on the self-determination, free will and the search for meaning. It is based on a series of philosophical-existential theses, proposing the research/ identification of the existential anxieties/ crisis and internal-ontological rebalancing/ rehabilitation through personal/ human growth and emancipation/ empowerment – solutions very useful also in humanistic social work practice/ evaluation and intervention, especially in the practice with clients with problems of adaptation and social integration (Krill, 1978).

*Gestalt psychotherapy/ intervention and positive psychotherapy/ intervention*

The gestalt psychotherapy proposes/ involves the achievement of the convergence between consciousness, experience and behavior, "between the figure and background"; emphases the importance, for the client, of being aware of what is *here* and *now,* and accepting the responsibility for his situation, while *positive psychotherapy* is based on the beliefs that all people are fundamentally good and they have the personal-constitutional capacity to be happy (Wheeler, 1991, p. 65).

Also, the *group methods and techniques* are increasingly used in humanistic social work. Especially in clinical social work are used, also, *the transactional analysis, psychotherapy focused on emotions, existential analysis, drama-therapy, dance therapy and movement therapy, art therapy, focusing, psychodrama,* etc.

## Appreciative Methods

Promotes, as objective, but also as the main strategy, the solving of social/ human problems through the appreciation, knowledge and increasing the optimistic, positive worker and client's expectations related to the client's evolution and the results of the intervention/ support activity (Bellinger, Elliott, 2011).

Operates with the conventional instruments of social work, like social inquiry, supervision, intervention project and case management, but are still resized by categories of the optimistic methods, and takes crucial paradigms from positive psychology, cognitive psychology or psychotherapy. The appreciative social inquiry respects some principles like the constructionist principle, of simultaneity, poetic principle, positive principle or of anticipation (Cojocaru, 2013).

## Balance Method

Is a humanistic method both of evaluation and intervention/ support/ care (Mc Call, 2001). In the humanistic social work practice it can operate with the following onto-balances:

- the balance of socio-affective onto-systems;

- the balance of socio-cognitive onto-systems;

- the balance of relationships and role-status onto-systems;

- the balance of attitudinal, cultural and spiritual onto-systems, etc. (Stefaroi, 2012).

## 3.1.4. Caring and Helping

Payne (2011) consider caring more important than helping. But he states that it is about of a holistic and humanistic caring, that includes the personality and spirituality, not only the physical and emotional spheres.

*"Humanistic social work focuses more than many models of social work practice on holistic caring processes rather than helping for two reasons. One is that many social work and similar services are involved in helping people with long-term-care needs; children whose parents cannot care for them; people with mental illnesses, intellectual, and physical disabilities; and older people. Therefore, social work requires more than a quick problem-solving intervention or social change and then standing aside; it requires developing the client's personal capacities to resolve difficulties and live an improved quality of life over a long-term involvement. Second, social work aims at psychological efficacy, as humanistic psychotherapies envisage, but it also involves a focus on empowering the social agency of social networks in the client's environment." (Payne, p. 139).*

To this end, in our opinion, it is essential that everyone who works, for example, in residential/ care institutions to meet a minimum conditions of human, educational, vocational, psychological or moral order. The organizations where they work must to be themselves a source of stability, efficiency and humanism for the customers (Stefaroi, 2007).

That because the empathetic ability, emotional wellbeing, happiness, personal development, altruism, agreeability, intelligence, culture, idealism, visionary orients the workers through the achievement of the humane/ humanistic goals of the care institution. The positive effects are felt over time particularly by shifting the focus from the care of body to the care of soul and personality.

### 3.1.5. The Role and Importance of the Humane and Spiritual Qualities of the Professional, as Basic Resources in Humanistic Social Work Practice

Because, in practice, from the humanistic social work principles and objectives perspective, between the practitioner's personality and the client's personality, especially in casework, in caring, therapy and education, is established a high psychological-ontological congruence (emotional, empathetic, humane, spiritual) the cultivation of the spiritual, humane and eudemonic-altruistic values and resources of the practitioner's personality and behavior must becomes an important theoretical concern.

To this end, the specific literature, from a postmodern and post-postmodern position, must promote an innovative approach on the professional's qualities and conducts, with a great attention paid to the humane and psycho-spiritual qualities such as empathy and compathy, spiritual welfare and virtue, happiness and eudemonic-altruistic energy/ motivation, personal development, humane develop-ment and humanity.

Therefore, the professional's humane personality should be considered the main resource of the humanistic social work practice, both when we pursue the psychological-eudaimonical objectives or the integrative, prosocial objectives.

It is, so, more than obvious the necessity of prioritization the development of the professional's psychological-ontological sphere, the axiological-moral/ prosocial sphere, the motivational-energetical sphere, with a great attention paid to the humane soul and spiritual soul; in conclusion to the humane personality.

Essential humane and spiritual qualities in working with the beneficiaries, such as empathy/ compathy, agreeability, tolerance, humanity, virtue, and other, are generated, largely, by the existence and manifestation of the humane personality, especially of the humane soul and spiritual soul, of course on the background and in the light of the overall personal, human and psychosocial development.

Through his humane personality, humane soul and spiritual soul, through the overall personal, human and psychosocial development, through his humane and spiritual qualities the professionals will send and stimulate the development of the humane and spiritual features at the customers too, factually sending to them positive energy, happiness, aesthetic, intellectual, spiritual, playful energy and qualities; thus contributing at their personal development, increasing the self-esteem, social consciousness, the capacity of initiative, social autonomy; will transmits empathy, humanity, agreeability, happiness and balance to the customers, will help, so, their personal/ human development, enhancing the positive perspectives of social reintegration and personal rehabilitation (Stefaroi, 2013).

# 3.2. Empathy and Compathy

## 3.2.1. The Importance of Empathy and Compathy in the Work of Professional

Empathy, this core psycho-spiritual, humane resource/ quality of the practitioner is a necessity in humanistic social work, but should not miss to any person acting in the overall social welfare/ work system (Gerdes, Segal, 2011).

Through empathy the worker's personality becomes sensitive to the sufferings and problems of the people in need, and, at the behavioral level, acquires agreeability (Hoffman, 2000).

Empathy is also a fundamental way of knowledge and representation/ evaluation to the customer and the environment in which it lives.

Through the empathetic and compathetic/ prosocial valences of the personality a worker from a residential institution for children, for example, can create a magical psychosocial and humane "universe" for satisfying the intimate, deep, emotional personal needs, can stimulate the spiritual growth and education, psychosocial and moral development of the children.

We can, so, to consider, the empathy and compathy, a benchmark of quality, and a necessary condition in the preparation, recruitment and evaluation of the personnel.


## 3.2.2. Personal-Psychological Sources of the Professional's Empathy and Compathy

The humane soul and humane ego are among the most important personality sources of empathy and compathy.

The professionals to whom the humane ego and humane soul are high developed acquires solidarist-humanistic qualities, traits such as empathy, agreeableness, tolerance etc.; the humane soul especially, having a determinant role in the formation of the humanistic, solidarist, humanitarian beliefs, convictions of the professional; also having a very important role in the orientation of the professional's character, in determining the attitudes towards themselves, towards work, people, values, society etc., towards the people in need and suffering, towards the client.

A crucial role in determining the empathetic/ compathetic valence/ dimension of the professional's personality and behavior it has the humane character, of course, on the background of its general personal and human development.

Only through the formation and establishment of the humane character is emphasized and highlighted the empathetic-humanist valence of the global personality and conduct, be set and manifest the personality as a structure expressly oriented towards the generalized other's jouissance, the personality that, by means of the system of prosocial/ humane skills, abilities and habitudes, is reflected in the professional's conduct and presence as a resource of jouissance for the good and socio-human fulfillment of the client, for the recovery, rehabilitation or mitigation of the customer's suffering.

The basic social factors of formation, development and support of the empathetic professional's personality, of the empathetic/ compathetic qualities and conducts, are the social environment, where he/she grew up or live, based on attachment, on solidarity and empathy/ compathy, the cultural education oriented to people and values, and the like (Stefaroi, 2013).

### 3.2.3. Empathy and Compathy as Core, Universal and Generic Qualities of the Professional in Humanistic Social Work Practice

Empathy is, theoretically, considered, in any form or view of social work, a core, universal and generic quality and resource of the professional, still is one of the underused therapeutic resources in practices (Rogers, 1959).

But humanistic social work gives its a crucial role.

In practice, empathy and compathy must to be represented and approached as phenomena and processes of very great complexity, depth and finesse, that involve the professional's personality and feelings and the client's personality and feelings, that involve, also, in the assistential/ therapeutic/ educational process, the persons and the group/ groups, the individual and the society, the group and the society, feelings and representations, values and beliefs, feelings and ideas, the material and spiritual existence.

That is the reason why the empathetic/ compathetic capacity and behavior is not an alternative, an option, but a consubstantial necessity of any profession on the social work field, particularly in the child welfare and social work, but also in the elderly and disabled.

Through empathy the worker's personality becomes sensitive to the sufferings and problems of the people in need, and, at the behavioral level, acquires agreeability (Gerdes, Segal, 2011).

In the assistential, therapeutic or educational process and phenomena the professional's empathy operates through its defining functions: cognitive, of communication and foresight, of emotional contagion and performance, of solidarity, prosocial, etc.

So, the empathetic capacity of the professional is a fundamental way/ means of knowledge and representation/ evaluation of the customer and the environment in which it lives, is a means of feel and emotional reflection of the client's feel and emotional state, therefore, is an emotional process; being also an interpersonal process is a social process, and, not least, a spiritual process/ phenomenon through the capacity of the professional's personality to resonate al the customer's culture and spiritual sensitivity.

In practice, in case work, in caring and education in a residential institution, the empathetic qualities of the workers are of great importance also in the goal regarding the organizational congruence, consistency, unity and functionality. In these institutions, the empathy must have a very important role. The professional-client inter-empathy has an undeniable curative function (Rogers, 1959).

The social care organization is a network of inter-empathies wherein, especially in children's institutions, the professional's personality can have a vital educational function.

The professional's personality interacts with all its physical, psychological, social, cultural, moral level and features, respectively:

- the personal characteristics - age, appearance, character, etc.;
- language;
- the specific cognitive and affective qualities;
- the system of values, sensibilities, tastes, habits, rules, customs, etc.;
- behaviors, gestures, activities, etc.


The organization/ institution of social care and education is so defined also by the personalities that compose it, including the professionals' personalities, with the three dimensions: affective, cognitive and spiritual.

In this end, the affective phenomena are in fact, relationships, interactions, compathies between the affective spheres of the persons, while the cognitive and spiritual phenomena are processes between its spiritual spheres. Of course, the compathetic interactions, processes and phenomena area of these organizations is infinitely large.

In an social institution, through the spiritual and social valences of the empathetic personality a worker can help to create a magical psychosocial and cultural "universe" for satisfying the intimate, deep, empathetic personal needs. For children, for example, the institution where they are temporarily placed is the place where is, still, built the ontological foundations of its personality, is the environment in which the is feed with spiritual and moral energy, it is the existential magic framework of training, existence and manifestation of his personality, of its happiness and soulful/ personal fulfillment. To this end, the role of the empathetic qualities of professionals is crucial (Stefaroi, 2013).

## 3.2.4. Activity Effectiveness and Achieving the Objectives

The researches and clinical evidences indicates that, in social work, as well as in other areas of social practices and interventions, psycho-therapy, education, and others, empathy is an innate human capa-bility of the practitioners and clients that can be used to increase the efficiency in both the eudaimonical-psychological and the integrative, prosocial objectives (Hoffman, 2000).

In humanistic social work the efficiency is high especially when it is considered the direct assistential/ therapeutic relationship between the professional and the client.

So, the professional, with the empathetic/ compathetic capacity of his personality and behavior succeeds to have a greater efficiency, both in the objectives involving the welfare and happiness of the client, as well as in those pursuing his empowerment, autonomization, socio-human integration.

Through the empathetic qualities/ capacity and resources of the personality, namely, the ability to feel the enjoyment (desires, sufferings) of the client, the ability to think and experience what the client thinks and feels, the ability to really sit in the client's place, to see the world as he/ she see it, the personal provision/ motivation to the other, sympathetic projection of the self, emotional-affective fusion, sympathetic intuition, identification with the client, transfer, etc. the practitioner acquires access to the customer's personality and subjectivity, and, also, acquires an effective method of therapeutic change.

So, without any doubt, the empathetic/ compathetic qualities of the professional, in any philosophy or theoretical orientation, form, doctrine of social work/ welfare constitute essential predictors of effectiveness and fulfillment of the objectives, the more in humanistic social work, where this quality of the professional exceeds the original psychosocial meaning, instituting also as a core value of the efficiency in practice (Gerdes, Segal, 2011).

The reason is that, in humanistic social work, by the empathetic resources of their own personality, the professional can engage most effective the resources for spiritual, eudaimonical and social rehabilitation of the customer's personality. Spiritual, eudaimonical and social rehabilitation being core objectives and efficiency indicators of this important path of social work at the beginning of the third millennium (Payne, 2012).

# 3.3. Spirituality and Virtue

## 3.3.1. The Importance of Spirituality and Virtue in the Work of Professional

Spirituality, the spiritual welfare, as state and latent resource, and the virtue, as (spiritual) energy and active resource, are others crucial personality resources and qualities of the worker, of great importance in humanistic social work practice.

So, the spiritual development/ sensitivity and virtue, as professional's qualities, resources, energies and conducts, may be considered important factors in the activity effectiveness and achieving the specific objectives of practice, especially in the activities with children, elderly and persons with disabilities, in casework, in caring, education, and therapy (Gilligan, Furness, 2006).

## 3.3.2. Spiritual Development and Sensibility

There are a number of personal/ personality traits/ characteristics such as aesthetic sensibility, idealism, optimism, faith, balance, beauty, belief, changelessness, positive thinking, moral power, pure consciousness, self-control, silence, simplicity, tolerance, trust, unconditional love, sincerity, stillness, soulfulness, cheerfulness, creativity, desirelessness, devotion, endurance, virtuous energy, enthusiasm, fearlessness, forbearance, forgiveness, freedom, honesty, hope, intuition, joy, mercy, patience, peace, perseverance, play, sweetness, tenderness, thoughtfulness, understanding, warmth, wisdom, happiness, interior comfort, irony, relaxed attitude towards life hardships and professional difficulties, which can be considered elements of the spiritual development and sensibility, as cardinal qualities and resources of the professional in humanistic social work practice, mostly in working directly with persons with disabilities, with children from residential institutions, elderly from residential institutions, persons with various forms of mental disorders, people with serious illnesses in terminal stages etc.

The reason is that, this traits, characteristics, qualities, resources, moral energies of the social worker, caregiver, educator, healthcare professional, psychologist etc, are important sources of the human/ humanitarian sensitivity, important sources of empowerment and eudaimonical rehabilitation of the person in suffering and difficulty.

In humanistic social work practice the relations with the client is not objectual but "spiritual". The term can help us to understand more deeply, completely and complex, the nature and specific of the professional-customer relationship.

Beyond the primary goal of social reintegration or economic rehabilitation, the customer expects also, from the professionals, related services such as tolerance, understanding, humor, aesthetics sensibility, morality, creativity, in a word, *spirituality* (Stefaroi, 2009b, p.174).

To this end, the recruitment activity of the professionals is designed so that the future employees to have the qualities that enable it to offer and such "services", of what often depends the success of the intervention. These qualities are key determinants of the professional's efficiency in humanistic social work practice.

Indubitable, the main source of these qualities is the professional's spiritual soul, with its main sub-spheres (the mystical soul, aesthetic soul, moral soul, intellectual soul etc.) on the background of the general personal and human development.

All of this works also to the development, formation and establishment of what we might call the virtuous personality, virtuous conduct, and the virtuous qualities of the professional such as virtue and moral will.

### 3.3.3. *Virtue and Moral Will*

The professional's spiritual qualities such as aesthetic sensibility, idealism, faith, balance, positive thinking, moral power, pure consciousness, self-control, tolerance, soulfulness, cheerfulness, creativity, desirelessness, devotion, endurance, virtuous energy, enthusiasm, fearlessness, forbearance, intuition, joy, altruism, empathy, mercy, patience, peace, optimism, perseverance, sweetness, tenderness, thoughtfulness, understanding, warmth, wisdom, relaxed attitude towards life hardships and professional difficulties, and more, cannot be explained only by the education, temperament or by the professional instruction but, mostly, by the degree of the effective presence of active culture and spirituality, of the projectivity and moral, aesthetic traits in the professional's personality, by the moral self and conscientiousness, by (spiritual) soul and character, generating this unique ancestral human existential phenomenon, this sacred aura of spirituality, ancestry and humanism of the person/ professional: **the virtue**.

Virtue having also an important spiritual-energetical function in the development and functioning of the prosocial professional's personality and behavior. The spiritual welfare and virtue instituting so as a very valuable resource of practice, of the professional's activity, of empowerment and enhancement/ improvement of the client's spiritual welfare and autonomy, also of enhancement/ improvement of the socio-moral relationships from the community (family, institution, organization, etc.) (McBeath, Webb, 2002).

Closely related to virtue, we bring to attention another important resource and quality of the professional in humanistic social work practice: **the moral will.**

Can be represented also as the phenomenon by which the humane ego tends to be updated; the humane conscience is the mental forum in which is performing this process. The more the humane ego is most developed the more the volitional capacity/ strength, the resistance to frustration, risk-taking, or the effort capacity/ strength of the professional are higher.

So, the moral will and the humane ego cooperates tightly in the personality formation, development and functioning, in the personal/ social efficiency, self-control, in the interpersonal behavior, in the current social/ professional activity (Sinnott-Armstrong, 2014).

All are crucial resources of the spiritual enthusiasm and virtuous energy, autonomy, self-regulating and self-development, social adjustment, personal fulfillment - crucial qualities of the professional (social worker, caregiver, therapist, educator, etc.) in humanistic social work practice, especially in working directly with:

- persons with disabilities;
- anomic and/or disintegrated families;
- children from residential institutions;
- elderly from residential institutions;
- persons with various forms of mental disorders, sick, etc.

### 3.3.4. Activity Effectiveness and Achieving the Objectives

As has been pointed, the importance of spirituality, virtue, moral will, as qualities of the professional's personality, is given by the fact that the relationship with the client is not objectual but "spiritual", and very complex (Berkowitz, 1996).

It is, so, impossible to imagine professional efficiency, in the jobs that involve working with people in need and suffering, without spirituality, virtue, culture, high moral will, with the soulful welfare and happiness state which it implies.

The studies and researches in the fields involving working with people concludes that the professionalism in these fields is strongly conditioned by the level of general personal and human development, including the degree of spirituality, virtue, moral will and "aesthetic" charisma of the person/ professional who provide social services.

In social work, usually, to the practitioners with high developed humane personality spirituality, as holistic traits of personality, the spiritual sensibility and virtue will be imposed as main factors of organization and holistic adjustment of the humanistic professional behavior, becoming a crucial attribute of the prosocial action/ activity and effective professional practice (Gilligan, Furness, 2006)..

Without virtue and spirituality the professional is under the dominion of selfishness, impulsiveness, personal undeveloped, laziness, lack of involvement, inactivity, inefficient professional behavior, dominating the defensive behaviors and non-involvement, sometimes even the aggressivity.

That is one of the reasons why the professional's virtue and spirituality becomes, in humanistic social work practice, important sources of efficiency and achievement of the assumed humanistic objectives, of change and empowerment to the people in need or suffering.

# 3.4. Happiness and Eudaimonic-Altruistic Energy/Motivation

### 3.4.1. The Importance of Happiness and Eudaimonic-Altruistic Energy/Motivation in the Work of the Professional

Although it may seem insignificant this quality is an essential humanistic resource of the professional in humanistic social work practice, especially of the practitioner (social worker, caregiver, therapist, educator, etc.) who works directly with the client.

That is the reason why happiness and eudaimonic-altruistic energy/ motivation, as professional's qualities, resources, energies and conducts, may be considered crucial factors in the activity effectiveness and achieving the specific objectives of practice, especially in casework, in caring, education, and therapy, in the activities with children, elderly and persons with disabilities, in the activities with sick people, and other.

## 3.4.2. The Happiness of the Client and the Happiness of the Professional

As was also emphasized in the paper, in humanistic social work practice between the practitioner's personality and the client's personality is established a high degree of emotional, empathetic, human, spiritual congruence.

This aspect highlights the importance of some socio-affective and eudaimonical interpersonal processes, where the conduct and interpersonal traits of the practitioner acquire therapeutic significance in both the integrative, prosocial objectives but also in those related to the psychological/ spiritual well-being of the clients (Jex, Gudanowski, 1992).

In this sense, there are a number of personal/ personality characteristics such as high level of personal fulfillment, interior comfort, altruistic motivation, irony, relaxed attitude towards life, hardships and professional difficulties, ie the soulful/ psychological welfare and happiness, which are crucial qualities in social work practice, because they are important source of the altruistic, prosocial energy and humane/ humanitarian behavior.

Important is the curative and eudaimonic relationship between the happiness of the client and the happiness of the practitioner.

The happiness and eudemonic-humane energy of the practitioner is a crucial factor in activity effectiveness and important resource in achieving the objectives in practice (Achor, 2010), especially in the activity with children, elderly, sick persons and with disabilities.

So, because one of the most important, constitutional objective of practice in humanistic social work is to enhancing the psychological welfare/ well being, the happiness of the beneficiaries, especially for children and the elderly, is very important to emphasize the aspect that one cannot speak about the clients' happiness and their rehabilitation in an environment where the personnel, employees, practitioners are unhappy, poor emotionally and eudaimonically.

### 3.4.3. *The Happiness and Eudaimonic-Altruistic Energy/Motivation of the Professional*

Humanistic social work promotes, after empathy/ compathy and spiritual welfare, the happiness and eudaimonic-altruistic energy/ motivation as core resources and crucial qualities of the professional in the specific practice, especially for the professionals who are in direct and prolonged contact with the customers (care personnel in institutions, foster parents, psychologists and others), indispensable resource of the altruistic and virtuous behavior, of the psycho-spiritual and humane qualities of the professional

This energy is able to contribute at the spiritual welfare or change to the distressed clients, permanent resource existing at the professional's personality level - resource afferent of an eudemonic-spiritual welfare and characterial structure constitutional oriented to the good of the other, to the common welfare and happiness.

In humanistic social work practice we speak about a kind of professional's happiness put into the customer's service, where the psychological-eudaimonical jouissance of the professional, reflected in the professional behavior, has a strong assistential and curative role.

To this and, the professional's altruistic and spiritual jouissance involves, in humanistic social work practice, at least, two major meanings:

- the jouissance related to higher, humane development of his personality, and

- the jouissance oriented towards the good of the client.

In the first case it is mainly about of a jouissance of the spiritual soul, of the higher consciousness, humane ego and character, and, in the second case, about a jouissance mainly of the humane soul, but also of the affective (social) soul, and of other prosocial formations, higher, humanized instances of the personality.

The soul, with all its areas and components, is the place and central source of the professional's humane jouissance, therefore, if in the case of the body, senses, instinct's jouissance we talk about libido and pleasure, in the case of soul's jouissance we talk about eudaimonia and happiness, and in the case of the humane soul's eudaimonia of happiness through the other, the client, or altruistic happiness of the professional.

Without a doubt, it is hard to speak of the professional's humane personality, humane behavior, humane and spiritual qualities in the conditions of a basal, elementary psychological jouissance, expressed in reactions, emotions and feelings predominantly conative, primitive, impulsive, based on the pleasure-pain hedonic-biological mechanism.

The professional's humane personality, humane behavior, the humane, moral, spiritual qualities of this, must have an interior psychological-eudaimonical correspondent, a jouissance to match. And so, in humanistic social work, we speak about *altruistic and spiritual happiness* of the professional.

Regarding the source of the professional's altruistic and spiritual happiness a crucial role it has the jouissance of the professional's soul, of the psychological-ontological sphere of his humane personality, the soul represented as a being which feeds, develop from/with virtue, from/with the good, welfare, happiness of the client.

At the process contributes also the professional's happiness onto-formation. The role and importance of the happiness onto-formation in the process of professional's development, in determining personality traits such as agreeableness, optimism, charisma, sociability, altruism, empathy is very important because it improves, elevates the jouissance, the interior subjective-experiential general state, causing the professional to feel fulfilled, authentically happy, or overflow of interior well, and to externalize, contaminating, affecting for better also the client, more unhappy, unfulfilled

The authentic happiness of the professional is derived from the spiritual/ soulful and human development, wellbeing and fulfillment as person and profession, as well as from the humane ego/ self development and fulfillment, because it is an eudaimonia of an psychological-ontological type, deeply, involving, holistically and trans-temporal, the personality as an all, is permanent, is a being, an existence, and not an emotion or pleasure of moment.

Thus, the professional's ego is not a contingent conative, autonomic, self-sufficient ego, subject of the organic fluctuations, of impulsivity, egotistic emotions, but an universalized, spiritualized, humanized, superised ego, the personality's eudaimonia of the professional involving, so, not only the resources of pleasure and jouissance of the self but the cultural resources of virtue and moral good of the entire humanity.

Results, from here, an humane energy, a happiness of the professional as a *human being*, a true happiness, an interior world and a psychological-spiritual, eudaimonical welfare that exceeds the personal need of internal homeostasical jouissance.

The surplus, thus, pouring in outside, in professional behavior, energy that reaches, so, also at the client, at the person in difficulty, through the altruistic, humane behavior of the practitioner, through charisma, agreeableness, transfer of spirituality, virtue and happiness.

In this sense, in humanistic social work practice, we can state that the professional's altruistic and spiritual motivational-energetic system is a superior ontogenetically construction within the general motivational system and overall personality of the professional, and it can be represented, succinctly, as *a set of energies associated of some motives, needs, trends, interests, intentions, aspirations, ideals of the professional that support the achievement, expression, disinterestedly, altruistic, compathetic of some professional behaviors, actions, facts, activities oriented towards the fulfillment of needs, desires, aspirations of the people in need or difficulty, of the client.*

It is an energy of the professional's humane personality - resort, factor, indispensable resource of the altruistic professional behavior, energy that not emerge from a circumstantial decision of the practitioner to contribute to the present welfare or change the person in difficulty, the, client but an energy, resource existing permanently at his whole being level, corresponding of an eudaimonical-spiritual welfare and motivational structure of personality constitutionally oriented towards the good/ welfare/ well being of the other, of the client.

In this case we must speak of an altruistic and spiritual motivational system of the professional, a superior ontogenetically construction within the general motivational system and global personality, and may be represented, succinctly, as a composition of motives, needs, trends, interests, intentions, aspirations, ideals of the person that support the realization, expressing, disinterested, altruistic, compathetic, of certain conducts, actions, facts, activities oriented towards the fulfillment of the needs, desires, aspirations of other people, of the clients, that support personal behaviors suitable to facilitate the spiritual, human, social development and welfare of the generalized other, social and eudaimonical rehabilitation of the individuals/ groups in need, suffering, in crisis, of the clients.

In this sense, one can speak, arbitrary of course, of two motivational-humane systems of the professional oriented towards the good of the other

1.  mobiles, needs, trends, interests, intentions, aspirations, ideals of the professional directly oriented towards the good of the client, sustaining the altruistic professional behavior of aid, support, care of the people in need, of the client, which we could tell *humane motivation of the professional of help and compassion*, and

2.  the system of mobiles, needs, trends, emotions, interests, intentions, aspirations, ideals of the professional that acts indirectly, axiological and energetical, as factors of guidance, spiritualization and humanization of the professional's behavior, generating the moral will and virtue, virtuous personality, charisma, humane authority - axiological-energical sources in the practitioner's action and conduct, of human, personal and eudemonical development and improvement of the client, through moral and spiritual virtue, transfer and compathy, of empowerment, emancipation, fulfillment of the persons in difficulty, socio-human, moral, eudaimonical degraded, of the client.

### 3.4.4. Activity Effectiveness and Achieving the Objectives

It is, so, impossible to imagine professional efficiency, in social work practice, and more so in humanistic social work practice, practically in all jobs that involve working with people in need and suffering, especially in the activities that involves children, elderly and persons with disabilities, in casework, in caring, education, and therapy, without qualities of the professional such spirituality, virtue, culture, but also without qualities of the professional such happiness and eudemonic-altruistic energy/motivation.

The literature concludes that the professionalism in working with people is strongly conditioned by the degree of happiness, enthusiasm, energy, optimism and charisma of the professional. The professional efficiency being correlated with the positive attitudes, with the degree of internal relaxation, the irony and personal happiness (Weisman, Nathanson, 1986, Bandura, 1986).

James (1981) believes that the job happiness/ satisfaction is the relationship between individual aspirations and achievements. At the same time, happiness is an onto-subjective psychological feature and it aprioristically guides the professional to performance.

We believe that the following professional's psychological-eudaimonical and motivational-energetical predispositions, qualities, states, personality configurations, situation stimulates the activity effectiveness and achieving the objectives in humanistic social work practice:

- authentic happiness, altruistic happiness;
- humane, altruistic motivation;
- eudemonic-altruistic energy;
- high level of personal fulfillment;
- interior comfort, irony, relaxed attitude towards the life, hardships and professional difficulties;
- soulful/ spiritual welfare;
- psychological-eudaimonical welfare;
- characterial structure constitutional oriented to the good and happiness of the other, to the common welfare;
- jouissance oriented towards the good and happiness of the client;
- positive emotions, feelings, thoughts, attitudes;
- the humane ego development and fulfillment;
- mobiles, needs, trends, interests, intentions, aspirations, ideals oriented towards the good of the client;
- professional and social satisfactions;
- relaxation, extraversion, democratic spirit, tolerance, epistemological and methodological flexibility, agreeableness, optimism, charisma, sociability, empathy, virtue;
- mature personality, emotional stability, self-control etc.

# 3.5. Personal Development, Humane Development and Humanity

### 3.5.1. The Importance of Personal Development, Humane Development and Humanity in the Work of the Professional

The activity of the professional in humanistic social work/ welfare "system" cannot be conceived without qualities such as personal development, humane development and humanity/ humanness/ kindness - very important resources and crucial factors of the activity effectiveness and achieving the objectives with all categories of clients and social problems, described in humanistic social work as *humane* problems, carried out by all categories of personnel.

Yet, these psychological and personological qualities are indispensable, especially, to the professionals who, through their work, involves in same time, indirectly, broad categories of problems and customers or having responsibilities of strategy, planning, supervision, management or training (Cross, 2001).

The personal development, humane development and humanity confers to professionals characteristics which helps to operate both with the soul and with the mind: would be perfect, so, as the manager, strategist and supervisor to meet all the personological, psycho-spiritual, humane qualities promoted by humanistic social work theory, axiology and methodology.

In humanistic social work "system" the supervision and management activities, for example, highlights the importance of the humanistic objectives, principles and values of the practitioners' practice, which the humanist supervisor/ manager/ coordinator must promotes in their specific activity, in the process of coordination, guidance, support, evaluation, monitoring. Are crucial in this sense their own qualities and behaviors, that need to excel through humane, empathetic, solidarist, altruistic, humanitaristic dimension, through humanity and personal/ human/ humane development.

From this point of view, the humanistic manager or supervisor is a model and source of conduct, education and human/ humane development of the professionals they coordinate or supervise; his personality is itself key-factor and source for personality and behavior development of the professionals, which, in turn, will transmits, further, the features/ qualities to the customers and social environments in which they directly operates through their interpersonal human/ humane qualities of conduct.

To this end, the manager/ supervisor's personality must be described through higher humanitarian personological qualifications of composition, structure and development, the humane, spiritual and moral sphere having high levels of development and dominant weight in the overall personality structure and composition, in the context of a very high moral and professional conscience, of a humanistic strong structured character, prosocial oriented, in the context of a very high development of the humanitaristic intellectual sphere.

In this sense, the professionals who through their work involves in same time, indirectly, broad categories of problems and customers or having responsibilities of strategy, planning, supervision, management or training, in humanistic social work system, besides the fact that it is characterized by personological qualities such as personal development, humane development and humanity/ humanness, is a humanist intellectual with vast and profound anthropological, philosophical, psychological, pedagogical, sociological, theological knowledge, the values and methods that it promotes relying on a good knowledge of the human condition, the man in general also as a person, of the human rights, of the human culture, the human history, of the human, social phenomena.

Of course, after all, and this knowledge are consubstantial and very important in the personal development process, in the humane development process, in profiling the holistic/ personological qualities such as humanity, humanness, kindness, humanitarism, etc. - crucial generic resources in humanistic social work practice.

## 3.5.2. Personal Development

It's hard to speak about the psychological, personological, humane and spiritual qualities of the professional from social work without refers to the concept and theory of *personal development.*

This quality brings to the professional's personality relief, complex and profound meanings, and integrates it into a comprehensive system of personality traits, represented by upper categories of evolution and orientation of the human being/ personality - thus imposing also a personological-humanistic and psychological-axiological approach not only the one instrumental and structural-functional (Cross, 2001).

In this way the humane and spiritual qualities of the professional in humanistic social work such as empathy, spirituality, or happiness are resignified and potentiated by the categories of personal development such as higher consciousness, complex and prosocial oriented cha-racter, self-control, realism, pragmatism, social skills, conscienti-ousness, strong will, high aspirations, personal autonomy, sociability, planning, culture, value etc.

In the scientific literature, the concept of personal development is associated or identified with a number of other concepts such as psychic development, growth, adaptation, social development etc.

It is a crucial category of the humanist-positive current from the social and human sciences, and, regarding the professional from the huma-nistic social work practice, implies, highlights, the following:

- High degree of awareness, self-knowledge, self-esteem (Maslaw);

- Maximizing and capitalizing of the internal potential of development, self-actualization, optimization, personal and social efficiency (Rogers);

- Psychological-emotionally well-being, satisfaction, happiness, hedonism (Seligman);

- Socio-emotional development, control of emotions, emotional intelligence (Erikson);

- Realism and balance;

- Powerful will, resistance to failure and frustrations;

- Hope, projectivity, orientation towards the future;
- Positive attitude, optimism, active thinking;
- Moral development;
- Aesthetic sensitivity;
- Maximal capitalization of the skills and talents;
- Professional development;
- Personal and social autonomy;
- Interpersonal development;
- Mature personality, adaptability;
- Overcoming the crisis, reducing the existential anxieties (Frankl).

Unquestionably, so, the humane and spiritual qualities of the professional in humanistic social work practice have much to do with the overall personal development. There were are combined the personal development with the spiritual development results a high level of humane development of the professional's personality, of humanism in thinking, attitude and conduct, of humanity.

### 3.5.3. Humane Development and Humanity

The humane development of the professional in social work is closely determined by the level of development of the humane soul, while the humanity, as synthetic and holistic qualities, involves also the humane conscience, humane character, humane ego, humane personality as a all, in the context of a high development of the global personality.

The professional's humane soul engages at a higher level, more complex, deeper and synthetic, the onto-formations from the professional's affective (social) soul and spiritual soul levels, generating the extraordinary ability of this to feel, live and think as a human being, as an ancestral being, as an exemplar humane being, but also as a *humane* being, by their ability to resonate, empathize, compathize with the human and spiritual experience of the other persons, of the client.

Through the great development of the professional's humane soul his personality as a whole is reformed and is defined through solidarist-humanistic qualities and behavioral traits such as empathy, agreeableness, tolerance, humanity, human sensitivity etc.

Thus, by the prosocial valences imprinted to professional's personality and behavior, the humane soul becomes, also, a crucial factor for his adaptation and social integration in the professional groups.

In this respect, the professionals' problems of adaptation, communication, integration, or the failure in working with the people in difficulty in groups, communities may also be interpreted as a result of the underdevelopment, disorders, injuries or weaknesses of his humane soul, and through the absence, or poor development, of some features as sociability, altruism, empathy, agreeableness, humane development, humanity - closely determined, therefore, by the level of development of the humane soul, but also by the level of development of the humane conscience, humane character, humane ego, humane personality as a all, in the context of a high development of the professional's global personality.

The most important factors in formation of the humane qualities of the professional are the social environment where it has been formed as personality and behavior, the social environment based on solidarity and empathy/ compathy, the cultural education oriented to people and values, the intellectual and of valorization capacity, the need for superior development and organization of the personality, the need for security, and, not least, the ontogenetic natural tendency of decentering of the self, of overall humanization of his personality and behavior, of socio-human integration and adaptation in groups and communities more and more complex on the course of his/her growing.

So, the "humanization" of the professional's personality and behavior is an emergent holistic and integrator process more pronounced at those who grow and live in social environment based on solidarity and empathy/ compathy, also at the professionals whose activity requires continuous and prolonged work with people in difficulty and/ or suffering, being achieved thus an adaptation of the professional's personality and behavior to the specific of activity, imposing, developing traits and qualities with a strong humanistic, humane prosocial, altruistic valence.

We can speak about a genesis of this qualities, about a structure, composition, organization, content, nature of the ontological-psychological resorts which determine it but the most interesting thing, in view of the theme regarding the humane and spiritual, personological and psychological qualities of the professional in humanistic social work practice, it is its prosocial, moral, compathetic, altruistic dimension.

The personological-humane qualities of the professional would not be possible without a strong cultural, anthropo-social, pan-human dimensioning. Therefore, this qualities operates by two complementary cardinal processes:

- one, oriented to himself, of humanization and universalization of the self, ego self-personality, and, another

- of cultural, anthropo-social setting, oriented towards other people, to world, society, values, to client.

This second dimension is the key driver for the imposing of the humane, prosocial behavior in practice.

In the humanistic social work practice perspective is more than obvious the need for prioritizing the development of this qualities. Professional's behaviors such as agreeability, tolerance, sociability and more, are generated, largely, by the existence and manifestation of his humane qualities, of course on the background and in the context of the global spiritual development, of the overall personal, human and psychosocial development.

To this end, the humanness/ humanity of the professional in practice must be defined closely related to the core values of humanistic social work/ welfare, mainly the representation of the man/ human as a supreme and benchmark value, and, therefore, of the client as a complex and spiritual human being (Arnet, 2011).

in this connection, the professional's humane qualities, virtue, and humanity are expressions of some personal constructs of a maximum complexity, generated by the presence of a mega-system which involve the person as a whole.

Thus, this professional's qualities are not mere expressions of the emotional and spiritual development, of the affective soul, of the spiritual and humane spheres, even if it involves and are fundamental, but also expressions of the:

- professional's general cultural development;
- existence of certain skills or inclinations;
- character development;
- eudaimonic-spiritual and eudaimonic-prosocial spheres;
- development of personality as a whole, through its humane orientation/ dimension, as a personality:
  - developed at a higher level, closer to the condition of human being of the person, as cultural, rational, spiritual and autonomous existence with its characteristic attributes - morality, virtue sociality, spirituality, personal development, adaptability and socio-human efficiency;
  - structured, through the soul, ego, conscience, character, motivation, skills, etc., so that to determine conducts oriented to the welfare of the other, of the generalized other, of the community, humanity, of the persons being in difficulty and/ or suffering, of the client.

The model of professional's personality in humanistic social work, capable of generating qualities such humanity, altruism, virtue, responsibility, generosity, patience, tolerance, consciousness is, so, the humane personality that combines the professional's global personality developed to a higher level with the personality so structured that determines effective professional conducts both in the objectives of personal empowerment and social integration, also in the ones of diminishing the client's suffering, or of happiness.

At the same time the model of professional's personality in humanistic social work, capable of generating qualities such humanity, altruism, virtue, responsibility, generosity, patience, tolerance, consciousness includes, in our opinion, and the professional's humane conscience and humane character.

The professional's humane conscience is an intellectual-axiological psychological universe, a superior moral instance, a psychological-personal place where faces, debate and builds the value systems, the conceptions towards himself, world, people, profession, society etc., the place of the professional's humanist ideals and beliefs, the place where are being built and develop the conceptions and attitudes towards people who suffer, in difficulty, the place where are being built and develop the humanitarian conceptions, attitudes and ideals.

So, when we speak about the professional's *humane* conscience, as important psychological-axiological source of his humane and spiritual, personological qualities, especially in humanistic social work, we keep in mind the prosocial, humanistic, solidaristic orientation of his global conscience, its humanistic general dimension, valence, oriented, by means of the own systems of values, concepts, attitudes, judgments, reflections, by his personal convictions and conceptions, to the good/ welfare of the other, of the generalized other, and, particularly, to the good of the client. It is about professional's convictions and conceptions as:

- man is the supreme standard of all values;

- all people are equal and have the right to happiness, dignity and personal fulfillment;

- happiness, dignity and social rehabilitation of the client are supreme values and objective of the professional activity etc.

In the same sense, the professional's humane (prosocial) character, too, as an important psychological-axiological source of his humane and spiritual qualities, is a holistic personality structure through which are formed and crystallized the personal features relating to the common good and jouissance, to all people, where these features are stated as constitutional qualities of the professional' conduct and activity. It's about character's traits such as:

- honesty;

- integrity;

- dignity;

- kindness;

- selflessness;

- respect etc.

One of the most important role of the professional's humane character, as structural formation of personality, is to conduct, with the contribution of the humane conscience and other psychological formations, including the humane ego, to the metamorphosis of the personality's humane and spiritual resources in proactive humanistic attitudes and traits. Only by the humane character is emphasized and highlighted the humanistic valence of the professional's conduct in social work practice.

Likewise, the professional's humane ego contributes to the establishment of his personal system of perceptual-attitudinal patterns, beliefs and assumed personal convictions, of the moral conduct, of the need for knowledge the human phenomenon, also contributes to the formation and establishment of the professional's humanistic devises and perceptual-attitudinal patterns, required in humanistic social work practice, like the following:

- I'm the man, the client is a man;

- 1 belong to humanity, the client belong to humanity;

- The clients well-being is also my well-being;

- I'm a good man, the client is a good man;

- I'm selfless, generous, the client is selfless, generous;

- I have dominant traits and conducts such as tolerance, compassion, humanness;

- I am happy through the happiness of the client.


Humanity, as fundamental, core, synthetic and holistic quality of the professional in humanistic social work, is strongly linked of the personality as a all, with all his spheres, levels, instances, functions and processes, but especially of the humane personality.

To this and, we can say that the professional's humane personality, in humanistic social work, is the ensemble of some constant humane psychological and behavioral characteristics highlighting, with preference, the aspects of:

- unity of the humane behavior in different professional situations;

- the dominance/ consistency of certain humanistic features, especially from the temperament and character spheres.

So, the professional's humanity, as core dimension of his humane personality, of his humane behavior, being of very high complexity, and having many dimensions, involves the two main orientations of the humanistic psychology regarding the personality:

- the "humanistic-positive" orientation, which focuses on personal development and social adaptation by using the psycho-volitional and adaptive resources, and

- the "humanist-ontological" orientation, that highlights especially the spiritual content of the self, the soul and the inner-ontological personality, the aesthetic, playful, moral or religious resources.

The "humanistic-positive" orientation highlight traits of the professional's humanity such as:

- high degree of awareness;

- self-knowledge;

- maximizing and capitalizing of the internal potential of development;

- self-actualization, optimization;

- personal and social efficiency;

- psychological-emotionally well-being;

- satisfaction, happiness, hedonism;

- socio-emotional development;

- control of emotions;

- emotional intelligence;

- realism and balance;

- powerful will;

- resistance to failure and frustrations;

- hope, projectivity;

- orientation towards the future;

- positive attitude;

- active thinking;

- moral development;

- maximal capitalization of the skills and talents;

- professional development;

- personal and social autonomy;

- interpersonal development;

- mature personality;

- adaptability.

The "humanistic-solidarist" orientation highlight traits of the humanity, as professional's quality in humanistic social work practice, such as:

- altruism;

- empathy/ compathy;

- attachment;

- love;

- dedication;

- spirituality;

- happiness;

- aesthetic sensibility;

- soulfulness, kindness;

- affection;

- benevolence;

- forbearance;

- gentleness;

- goodness;

- grace;

- graciousness;

- hospitality;

- patience;

- sympathy;

- tenderness;

- tolerance;

- understanding;

- amiability;

- beneficence;

- charity;

- clemency;

- consideration;

- delicacy;

- helpfulness;

- indulgence;

- philanthropy;

- serviceability etc.

Involving, so, two main orientations, humanity, as fundamental, core personality resources of the professional in humanistic social work is however a unitary, synthetic and holistic quality, bringing together both sets of traits, afferent to the concept of humane personality. To this end, the professional's humane personality, as the main source of the professional's humanity/ humanness, may be described as a set of onto-formations, such as soul, humane self, humane consciousness, humane character, and others - structural onto-psychological and intellectual sources, as well as the overall humane valence, dimension of the professional's global personality, meaning kindness, goodness, altruism, personality opened to the overall manhood jouissance, increased sensitivity to the other's suffering - itself, but also emergent resource of empowerment, wellbeing and happiness for the people from ambience; both being foundations/ explanations of the professional's humane qualities, to humanity as cardinal personality resources in humanistic social work practice.

In conclusion, also the humanity, as emblematic quality of the professional in humanistic social work, are revealed by two key explanations:

- as a result of the personality developed at a higher level, the most high, the most close to the condition of human being as autonomous cultural, rational, spiritual existence, and with its characteristic attributes - morality, virtue, sociality, spirituality, personal development, adaptability and socio-human efficiency,

- as personality structured through soul, self, conscience, character, motivation, skills, etc. so that determines conducts oriented towards the wellbeing of the generalized other, towards the common good, to humanity, and dominant traits such as empathy, altruism, generosity, kindness, etc.

## 3.5.4. Activity Effectiveness and Achieving the Objectives

Personal development, humane development and humanity, practically all the qualities enumerated above, a necessary, even crucial, in humanistic social work practice, regarding the activity effectiveness and achieving the objectives, because the practitioner not only provide simple compensatory aid, does not work only for the customers' survive, but seeks to relieve the client suffering, and change his socio-human condition through his humane presence, through its personality's altruism and optimism, through its opened mind and soul, through its humanity.

Are crucial in this sense their own humane behaviors that need to excel through empathetic, solidaristic, altruistic dimension, through agreeableness and charisma. From this point of view, the humanistic practitioner is a model and source for the personality and behavior development of the customers. To this end, the practitioner's personality must be described through higher qualifications of composition, structure and development. The humane sphere and dimension have a high levels of development and dominant weight in the overall personality structure and composition, in the context of a very high moral and professional conscience, of a humanistic strong structured character, prosocial oriented.

In this sense, the activity effectiveness and the achievement of the objectives are directly proportional with the weight of the humane sphere and dimension in the overall personality structure and composition, with the presence of some professional's qualities such as morality, virtue, sociality, spirituality, personal development, adaptability, empathy, altruism, generosity, kindness, etc.; in some crucial words: personal development, humane development and humanity.

In works as strategy, management, supervision the activity effectiveness are crucial determined of this professional's qualities and behaviors, that need to excel through humane, empathetic, solidarist, altruistic dimension, through agreeableness and charisma. From this point of view, the humanistic professional is a model and source of education and humane development of the staff, his personality being key-factor and source for personality and behavior development of other professionals from the professional collectivity (Cross, 2001).

The strategist, manager, supervisor, educator, in humanistic social work system, is a humanist intellectual with vast and profound anthropological, philosophical, psychological, pedagogical, sociological, theological knowledge, the values and methods that it promotes relying on a good knowledge of the human, social phenomena, of the man in general also as a person, as individual, of the human rights culture.

Aiming the maximization of the activity effectiveness, the humanistic strategist, manager, supervisor, educator, as model and sources for other professionals, must to work, with his humanity, personal and humane development, with his all knowledge, experience, soul and personality, at the formation and development of the professional and humane personality of the worker, of his professional attitudes and behavior, expressed in qualities of personality and conduct as conscientiousness, accountability, empathy/ compathy, agreeableness, happiness, personal/ human development, altruism, optimism, tolerance, etc. The aspect highlighting the crucial rol of education in forming and developing of the humane and spiritual qualities of the professional in humanistic social work practice, which explain the activity efficiency not only by the qualities of the soul, but also by qualities of the intellect, acquired through culture and education. Whether these qualities are of the caseworker either of the strategist, ultimately, their mediated effect, through behavior and charisma, in practice, will be seen in the social and psychological rehabilitation of the person in need and distress, of the client.

## 3.6. Humane and Spiritual Qualities of the Professionals in Humanistic Social Work Practice

### 3.6.1. Humane and Spiritual Qualities of the Social Worker

In humanistic social work the social worker is a humanist intellectual with vast and profound anthropological, philosophical, psychological, pedagogical, sociological, theological knowledge, the values and methods that he promotes relying on a good knowledge of the human, social phenomena (Payne, 2011).

With his qualities, knowledge, experience, soul, personality and behavior the social worker operates for the formation and development of the client's humane and prosocial personality, for formation and development of his optimistic and prosocial attitudes, expressed in conducts and qualities of personality as adaptability, conscientiousness, accountability, balance, diligence, happiness, virtue – qualities of the personality and conduct that would facilitates the personal and social rehabilitation of the client in humanistic social work/ welfare "system".

Among the international definitions given to the profession of social worker, closest of its representation through the categories of humanistic social work, we mention, in its original form, the one offered by *The International Federation of Social Workers (IFSW)*.

*The social work profession facilitates social change and development, social cohesion, and the empowerment and liberation of people. Principles of social justice, human rights, collective responsibility and respect for diversities are central to social work. Underpinned by theories of social work, social sciences, humanities and indigenous knowledge, social work engages people and structures to address life challenges and enhance wellbeing (ifsw.org/g).*

As can be seen, emphasis is placed, in the social worker's activity, on change, development and empowerment, lofty goals that request superior personal qualities from him.

The humanness/ humanity, empathy, virtue, altruistic motivation, therefore the essential psychological-spiritual and humane traits, qualities and resources in humanistic social work practice, should not miss to any social worker, regardless of the category of beneficiaries or the administrative level in which it operates, but are crucial in their entirety, at the social workers that, more or less directly, are connected or contribute in making decisions regarding the welfare and destiny of people in difficulty and suffering as children, elderly, disabled, institutionalized persons (Shebib, 2002).

### 3.6.2. Humane and Spiritual Qualities of the Psychologist

Regarding the behavior, activity and objectives of the psychologist in humanistic social work, the psychological, spiritual and humane qualities such as empathy and compathy, spiritual welfare and virtue, happiness and eudemonic-altruistic energy/ motivation, personal development, humane development and humanness play a crucial role, are actually some inexhaustible resources, but mostly a therapeutic mobiles, with which the humanistic psychologist achieves their specific objectives in the multidisciplinary team.

In this regard, the psychologist's personality or its spiritual qualities shall be described in terms of:

- complex personality;
- exceptional spiritual traits;
- soul, empathy;
- spiritual welfare and happiness;
- spiritual/ humane sensitivity;
- agreeableness, charisma (Shebib, 2002);
- culture and humane intelligence.

Both, the psychological assessment and the humanistic intervention start from the truth that the greatest problem for the customers is nor the retard of cognitive development, nor the repressed sexual experiences in the early childhood but their soul, personality and human relationships destroyed by unfavorable social and institutional circumstances, including those from protective system.

Therefore, in the theoretical foundation of its work, the humanistic psychologist/ psychotherapist uses all psychological theories and paradigms, is open to all theoretical models –psychological, philosophical, anthropological, sociological, biological, theological, aesthetical, sociological, mystical, using his scientific knowledge and training (Madanes, 2006), but especially the virtues of his humane personality, the psychological-spiritual and humane qualities: empathy and compathy, spiritual welfare and virtue, happiness and humanness/ humanity.

## 3.6.3. Humane and Spiritual Qualities of the Caregiver, Therapist, etc.

Regarding the psychological-spiritual, humane qualities of the caregiver or of other workers directly being in connection with the clients, among the qualities brought to attention in this paper, namely empathy and compathy, spiritual welfare and virtue, happiness and eudemonic-altruistic energy and motivation, personal development, human development and humanness/ humanity, probably spiritual welfare and virtue, happiness and eudemoc-altruistic energy and motivation, empathy and compathy are further required.

The reason is that, unlike, for example, the human development and humanness, that are resources, qualities largely passive, of background of the personality, spiritual welfare and virtue, happiness and eudaimonic-altruistic energy and motivation are active resources, inter-personal, "substances" of the daily communication and interaction with the beneficiaries of the social assistance services, especially in residential institutions, foster families, etc.

Empathy, as core psycho-spiritual, humane resource/ quality of the professional in general humanistic social work, is a consubstantial necessity of the caregiver, therapist, etc., especially in working with children, elderly sick persons. Through empathy the caregiver, therapist's personality becomes sensitive to the sufferings and problems of this people. Empathy being also a fundamental way of its knowledge and evaluation.

Through the empathetic and compathetic/ prosocial valences of the personality a caregiver or therapist from a residential institution for children, for example, can create a magical psychosocial and humane "universe" for satisfying the intimate, deep, emotional personal needs, can stimulate the spiritual growth and education, psychosocial and moral development of the children (Fox, 2011).

A other crucial quality very important in the caregiver and therapist's activities is spirituality. The spiritual development/ sensitivity and virtue, as caregiver and therapist's qualities, resources, energies and conducts, may be considered important factors in the activity effectiveness and achieving the specific objectives of practice, especially in casework, in caring, education, and therapy (Wolgin, 1997),.

There are a number of personal/ personality traits/ characteristics such as aesthetic sensibility, idealism, optimism, faith, balance, beauty, belief, changelessness, positive thinking, moral power, pure consciousness, self-control, silence, simplicity, tolerance, trust, unconditional love, sincerity, stillness, soulfulness, cheerfulness, creativity, desirelessness, devotion, endurance, virtuous energy, enthusiasm, fearlessness, forbearance, forgiveness, freedom, honesty, hope, intuition, joy, mercy, patience, peace, perseverance, play, sweetness, tenderness, thoughtfulness, understanding, warmth, wisdom, happiness, interior comfort, irony, relaxed attitude towards life hardships and professional difficulties, which can be considered elements of the spiritual development and sensibility, as cardinal qualities and resources of the caregiver/ therapist in humanistic social work practice (Shebib, 2002, Payne, 2011, Stefaroi, 2013).

The reason is that, this traits, characteristics, qualities, resources, moral energies of the caregiver, educator, healthcare professional, therapist etc, are important sources of the human/ humanitarian sensitivity, important sources of empowerment and eudaimonical rehabilitation of in casework, caring, therapy or education.

Alongside empathy and spirituality, the happiness and eudaimonical-altruism have a great contribution in increasing the efficiency of the therapist and caregiver, in the perspective of the humanistic social work practice values and objectives.

This quality is an essential humanistic resource of the caregiver, therapist, educator, etc., in casework, caring, therapy, education. That is the reason why happiness and eudemonic-altruistic energy/ motivation, as worker's qualities, resources, energies and conducts, may be considered crucial factors in the activity effectiveness and achieving the specific objectives of practice, especially in the activities with children, elderly and persons with disabilities, in the activities with sick people, and other.

### 3.6.4. Humane and Spiritual Qualities of the Manager and Supervisor

Instead, for the manager, strategist and supervisor engaged especially in leadership, planning, monitoring and mentoring activities, are useful, especially, qualities such as personal development (Lilienthal, 1967), human development and humanity. The personal, human/ humane development and humanity anyway encompasses also the others, and confers to managers, supervisor's personality and behavior those characteristics which help to operate both with the soul and with the mind.

In humanistic social work system the activity of supervision highlights the importance of humanistic objectives, principles and values of the worker's practice, which the humanist supervisor it promotes in his specific activity, in the process of guidance, support, evaluation, monitoring. Are crucial in this sense their own qualities and behaviors, that need to excel through humane, empathetic, solidarist, altruistic dimension, through agreeableness and charisma.

From this point of view, the humanistic supervisor is a model and source of education and human development of the professionals they supervise, his personality is itself key-factor and source for personality and behavior development of the professionals that it supervises.

To this end, the supervisor's personality must be described through higher qualifications of composition, structure and development (Kadushin, Harkness, 2014). The spiritual and moral sphere have high levels of development and dominant weight in the overall personality structure and composition, in the context of a very high moral and professional conscience, of a humanistic strong structured character, prosocial oriented.

Also, the supervisor, in humanistic social work system, is a humanist intellectual with vast and profound anthropological, philosophical, psychological, pedagogical, sociological, theological knowledge, the values and methods that it promotes relying on a good knowledge of the human, social phenomena, of the man in general also as a person, as individual, of the human rights culture.

Therefore, based on the theoretical, axiological and teleological framework of humanistic social work, besides the universal tasks and activities, the role of the humanistic supervisor is to guide, help, educate, monitor, control, check the professionals' activity so that these ones to can contribute at the fulfilling the assumed humanistic mission of the specific practice.

In this end, the humanistic supervisor, must to work, with his knowledge, experience, soul and personality, at the formation and development of the professional and humane personality of the worker, of his professional attitudes and behavior, expressed in qualities of personality and conduct as conscientiousness, accountability, empathy/ compathy, agreeableness, happiness, personal/ human development, altruism, optimism, tolerance, etc.

Only to the extent that the supervised professionals will acquire/ develop these traits and behaviors, as a result of supervision activity, the supervisor may consider performing his educational task. The aspect highlighting the crucial educative dimension of the supervision in humanistic social work, the essential rol that the supervisor plays, not only as a simple functionary but rather as a man with a big heart, developed moral personality, as a model, as an educator, as a great character.

In the humanistic social work system supervision is also an administrative and educational process, used in institutions and services of social work and social care, in order that the workers to perfect the practices and activities of empowerment and care the customers, to develop the socio-human abilities, of communications/ socialization, to increase the humanistic knowledge of the professionals so that these to can provide high-qualities services.

To this end, the promoting of the humanistic theoretical and practical knowledge regarding the customer as human being and personality and not as a non-functional element of a social system is a great task of the humanist supervisor, purpose in which also their own psychological-spiritual, humane qualities as empathy and compathy, spiritual welfare and virtue, happiness and eudemonic-altruistic energy and motivation, and, especially, personal development, human/ humane development and humanness/ humanity are very useful.

## 3.7. Humane and Spiritual Qualities and Conducts of the Professional in Child and Family Humanistic Social Work

If there is an area of practice where are required, without exception, all the humane and spiritual qualities and resources of the professional's personality and conduct, then that area is the child and family humanistic social work.

In this sense, the professional, in family and child humanistic social work, is not a mere functionary which identify, bureaucratically, some malfunctions and tries to solve them in order of a merely technical recovery, simple restoration of the original family functioning, but seeks to identify also the human, spiritual, cultural, moral problems facing the family members (American Humane Association, 2004).

The reason is that most of the problems confronted by the families are linked to its moral and human degradation, to its moral and human anomies. The dissolution of the family moral and human values has, as a result, the disaggregation, loss of the unity, solidarity, and common values. The process has dramatic consequences for children, the elderly, the sick, who are usually dependent of the family internal resources, of the unconditional support of the others (Jones, 2014).

To succeed the improving of the human and moral climate from these families and reducing the negative impact on their members the main task of the services and professional's activity is that to transform the precarious interpersonal relationships in *humane* and morale relationships, starting from the idea that the human suffering, unhappiness, personal failure, loss, dehumanization of the individual an community have, largely, the sources in the precariousness social and moral relationships.

The professional's personality and its psychological-spiritual qualities represents, for this purpose, the means, the essential professional resource that can facilitate the achievement of the objectives in practice in child and family humanistic social work.

The professional's humanistic activity, its psychological-spiritual qualities and humane quality and behavior, can facilitate the family change, can humanize the troubled social relationships, the dehumanized, dysfunctional micro-community, the moral, psychological damaged people, in difficulty, suffering, conflict, underdevelopment, reaching so to perform the specific mission, to determine the family changes regarding his moral and human climate.

In this process the humanistic practitioner is involved with whole its self, soul, intellect and experience, in the complex assembly of relationships, connections, conflicts, attachments, inter-empathies, compathies, feelings, passions, loves, projects, dramas of the family group with problems, detecting the dysfunctions, problems, underdevelopments, anomalies, building the diagnostic by an etiology and phenomenology of moral and human type, focusing, therefore, on *highlighting the dysfunctions from the human relations level,* the intervention aiming to convert them, by means of the knowledge, experiences, humane personality, soul, and psychological-spiritual qualities of the professionals from the team intervention, in *humane* and moral relationships, determining improvements, impressive qualitative changes at the family level as a whole, as well at the level of each member of the family; the transformative process evolving in cascade, involving humanizing sub-processes at all levels, eliminating many dysfunctions, disorders, problems, sufferings; the new created family climate being defined by qualifiers such as harmony, morality, solidarity, altruism, compathy, responsibility, cooperation.

This climate will imposes, ultimately, as a curative solution for many family problems, and only to the extent that the professionals and social services succeeded to determine it, with their qualities, activities, measures, conducts can sustain that they operates thoroughly and efficiently, and meet their specific mission in community.

Likewise, the role of the professional is mainly that, through and with his personal knowledge and qualities such as empathy and compathy, spiritual welfare and virtue, happiness and eudemonic-altruistic energy/ motivation, personal development, human development and humanity, to educate and empower the family to manage its life in such a way that to prevent the disaggregation, the conditions that lead to processes of moral, human, cultural, spiritual degradation, to high sufferings and serious difficult situations, of the family as a whole, or of the members, with an emphasis on children (Gammer, 2008).

Should also be noted, the practice, the conduct of the professional in child and family humanistic social work, in the evaluation activity, care, education, therapy, case management, in designing and application of the intervention project, must be carried with much professional discipline and scientific rigor.

In this sense, one can state that, the humanistic professionals from the institutions for children, those who have in placement children at home, the professionals who works with families and children in need in various authorities, public or private organizations, are first, and foremost, of course, persons with great soul, but also with a very rigorous scientific and professional training. Their humanistic professional behavior combining so in an effective way the sentiment with the information, the soul with the intellect, the humane personality with the intelligence and social/ professional experience.

In child and family humanistic social work practice empathy, as professional's quality, is a crucial resource that can be used to increase the efficiency in both the psychological and the integrative, prosocial objectives. The efficiency being high especially when it is considered the direct assistential/ therapeutic relationship between the professional and the child, or family.

Regarding the importance of spirituality and virtue, as qualities of the professional's personality in activity effectiveness and achieving the objectives in working with children and families, this is given by the fact that, in her deep and authentic nature, the relationship with the child or parent is not objectual but "spiritual", and very complex, and therefore the dominant resources involved must be of this nature.

That is one of the reasons why the professional's virtue and spirituality becomes, in family and child humanistic social work practice, important sources of efficiency and achievement of the assumed humanistic objectives, of psychological and social change, rehabilitation and empowerment of the child, or of the family as a whole.

Very important are, also, in family and child humanistic social work, qualities as happiness, altruistic motivation, personal development, humane development and humanity, because the practitioner, in working with children or families, not provide only simple compensatory aid but seeks to relieve and change their psychological and social condition through its *humane* presence, through its personality's happiness, altruism, charisma, through its personal development, humane development and humanity.

The aspect highlighting the crucial role of the education/ training in forming and developing of the humane and spiritual qualities of the professional who will work in family and child social work/ welfare system. In this sense, on the background of these psychological-personal qualities, a social worker or psychologist, a caregiver or manager, in family and child social work areas, the activity must be performed with much professional discipline and scientific rigor, the practitioner being first, and foremost, of course, a person with a great soul, but also with a very rigorous scientific and professional training. Their humanistic professional activity combining so, especially in working with children, in an effective way, the sentiment with the information, the soul with the intellect, the humane personality with the professional experience, the professional behavior with the *humane* behavior.

# PART III
## (Appendix)
## IDEAS, FRAGMENTS, ELEMENTS
## OF SOME NEW PAPERS (in working)
## IN THE
## *HUMANISTIC SOCIAL WORK*
## PROJECT

# Appendix 1

# "HUMANISTIC SOCIAL WORK:
## The THIRD WAY in Theory and Practice"

*As philosophy and theory, humanistic social work, as the third way, is a conglomerate of theories, paradigms, orientations, but which have some crucial ideas as vectors: the person/ client as human being, with sentiments, soul, personality, desires, sufferings, needs of love, needs of happiness and accomplishments, emphasis on personality, human relations and micro-community as basic resources of practice, positive, optimistic and appreciative expectation in practice, person-centred and community-centred approach in evaluation and intervention, concentration on the future and not on the past, the human rights, social justice, a humanistic perspective on the practitioner and his conducts in practice.....................................................*

*.........................................................*

*Theoretically and methodologically, social work, in general, is based on the resources of social and human sciences, philosophy and other areas of the science and practice. This is one of the reasons why the theory and practice of social work are so complex and full of dichotomies and doctrinal or methodological contradictions, taking, so, from these the majority theories and tools of practice, but and the theoretical/ doctrinal debates regarding the relationship between individual and society, freedom and responsibility, matter and spirit, structure and element, individualism and solidarity, stagnation and change (through evolution vs. revolution), the issue of individual and collective rights, etc.*

*Practically, the theory and practice of social work comes from behind, from the past, assimilating them, usually afterwards, and adapting them to the specific purpose, mission and methods. Thus, these determine the specific epistemology and methodology of social work to include, harmonious or dichotomous, orientations, ways, perspectives and theories of the whole areas of contemporary philosophy and socio-human sciences: phenomenologist, existentialist, feminist, post-modern, structuralist, behaviorist, psychoanalytic, psychosocial, cognitivist, holist, functionalist, criticist, traditionalist, radical, constructivist, humanist, etc. And the list could continue more.*

*Yet, at a first glance, social work, as theory and practice, is dominated by two, relatively opposed, major ways, forces, orientations, namely Traditional or Conventional Social Work and Radical or Critical Social Work. The theoretical and doctrinal debate between the two constitutes subject of many books, articles and studies.*

*Traditional or Conventional Social Work is the starting point in any theoretical and ideological discussion regarding the values, mission and methods of the social work, both chronological and axiological-methodological considerations, for the simple reason that it is the first and original form, but also because it provides the fundamental system of values and purposes of the social work/ welfare practice. Human/ social solidarity, redistribution, sensibility and caring for the other's welfare are universal values and objectives of the social work, anytime and anywhere.*

*Biestek (1978), defines the traditional social work especially through the following key values and principles: individualization, acceptance, tolerance and nondiscrimination, non-judgemental attitude, confidentiality and respect for client as a person. So, Traditional Social Work is less interested in the social, economic or political context, which determine or support the social problems, or in the structural socio-political progress or change, which could lead to the elimination or reducing problems, the focus is on the needs and feelings of the individuals/ clients, considering each client as a unique person, each individual must to be treated as a unique human being and not just as a structural member of a community, group or society.*

*The traditional social work practice is much indebted to the civic sense of people, sense of unity and appurtenance to the human species, to the specific moral and religious practices and values from the religion or culture in which it applies. Care theory and humanitarian theory, mainly, underlying the traditional or conventional social work's epistemology. The practitioners meet, with preference, the roles of caregiver, counselor/ therapist, facilitator, broker and evaluator.*

*Traditional Social Work practice is, but, accused to an attitude of condescension and contempt towards its clients, while the traditional social worker is considered an indispensable tool of the ruling classes from capitalist society. The promoters of Radical and Critical Social Work states that the undeclared its mission is, in fact, to contribute at the maintaining of the capitalist state order, and therefore, at the social and economic polarization, social, institutionalized, systematic and internalized oppression, social injustice and other chronic/ structural societal anomalies.*

*Critical and Radical Social Work. The main purpose of this contemporary perspective on social work, philosophy and policy, is to move away from the traditional approaches, that were based on a medical and emotional model of the man, that places people in a passive position, with the focus on the person (especially on the material and emotional needs) rather than on the society and community as a whole, on the structural and systemic level, from where, according to the theoreticians of Radical and Critical Social Work, derived the social and human problems.*

*Thus, through its constitutional nature Radical/ Critical Social Work is established and as a response and critical attitude, even revolutionary, against traditional/ conventional social work, promoting values, categories or practices such as: social change and community empowerment, structural social work, social justice, anti-oppression policies, radical changes.*

*If Traditional/ Conventional Social Work focuses the concern on the person welfare, here and now, in Critical/ Radical Social Work the emphasis falls on the determination of some systemic structural transformations and changes so that the welfare to be derived from the optimal socio-economic structure/ constitution and the social justice, ontological-functional established. The practitioner being, thus, interested to a deserved and enduring welfare, with respect for the fundamental values of human dignity and rights, obtained both through social progress and change as well as through empowerment. In the current activity of the practitioner the client is encouraged to claim and acquire its legitimate and fundamental rights, and not to be at the mercy of others, or to beg help. The practitioner meets in this case, largely, the roles of advocate, enabler, negotiator and mediator.*

*Heavily, the critical and radical theories, the theories of social change and progress (hegelian, marxist, structuralist, feminist), the anti-discriminatory and anti-oppressive theories, post-colonial and new-structural theories underlying, epistemologically, this paradigm of social work.*

*The major issues which aims to approach and solve are the greatest social and human problems of the society, mainly the poverty, economic and social polarization, social exclusion, discrimination, abuse, etc; focusing therefore to the structural inequalities and the oppressed/ marginalized practices and politics, promoting a determinist-holistic representation of the causes and factors that generate and maintain the social problems; therefore has a systemic-societal approach to the welfare system, operating, at the philosophical level, with the structural-functionalist paradigm in problems solving; the welfare being associated with the achievement of certain fundamental societal and political changes. In this regard, the social workers must work collectively, helping people to deal collectively with social problems, white the capitalist injustice and oppression... ... ... ... ... ...................*

*... ... ... ... ... ... ... ...........................................*

*In the last decades another orientation, in a subtle manner, gradually, seems to impose with increasing force. It's about the humanistic orientation and the logical expression, formed and enforced fairly recent and prudent in the specific literature: Humanistic Social Work. Syntagm, theory and methods that are in process of establishing and remains to be seen whether they will get to sit alongside Traditional Social Work and Radical Social Work, alongside their theories and methods, and especially if it will impose, in a coherent way, in the current practice of the professionals and agencies.*

*The process is closely related to the offensive of humanistic psychology and psychotherapy, on the one hand, and microsociology and humanistic sociology, on the other hand. All in the context designed by the phenomenology, existentialism and postmodernism/ post-postmodernism in the social theory and practice areas.*

*The abundance of concepts and theories, methods and techniques from humanistic psychology and psychotherapy, humanistic sociology and microsociology justify the observation that we can be, already, in the presence of a third way in social work, with almost certain perspective to become dominant in the future.*

*The explanation is found in the fact that humanistic social work incorporates concepts and methods from the two established stances, but also brings many new elements, according to the new social, human, economic, cultural realities and trends, and the new achievements in science and practice. In this way, in addition, it can be stated that humanistic social work could become one of the most important doctrinal/ methodological solution for many social and human problems at the beginning of the third millennium.*

*The necessity of a humanistic approach in social work, with emphasis on the theories and practices of empowerment (persons and communities) and empathy (as means of socio-human solidarity and therapeutic relation), became evident especially after the fall of communism in Central and Eastern European countries, which collapsed several aspirations to achieving a society without inequality and oppression and with the advent of the economic crisis, which reduced many resources with whom to be helped the vulnerable peoples, individuals and social groups in need or difficulty, through the redistribution arrangements and social control, shocking seriously the welfare state.*

*The two major social, political and economic events have heavily affected the ontological and ideological foundation of the radical social work (anti-communist revolutions) and of the traditional social work (economic crisis). Such, has been greatly affected the project of the structural social and political change, the construction of a society without oppression, social injustice, inequality, discrimination and poverty, especially through socio-political progress, radical change, promoted by the radical/ critical/ structural social work, and of helps the vulnerable groups, individuals/ people in need, in suffering, through welfare state and social solidarity within capitalist society, promoted by traditional/ conventional social work.*

*The "humanistic social work" concept attempts to meets and organize, epis-temological-methodological, the humanistic theory and methodology from the contemporary social work, into system, giving both a unitary theoretical and methodological framework and a forum for debate and professional or scientific innovation. Personal and socio-human development, participation, action, attachment, empathy and happiness theories, appreciative methods, humanistic psychotherapies and existential analysis are the theoretical and methodological bases of the policy and practice of the third way/ orientation in social work and social welfare.*

*Humanistic paradigm, which, up to a point, is identical with the social work as a whole, highlights, according to the most important orientations of humanistic thought, the following fundamental types of ideas and concepts:*
- *Promotion the concrete and complex human being, the individuality and personal happiness, its fundamental interests, feelings and values, the spiritual well-being of the person;*
- *Personality and empathy like the fundamental resources of practice;*
- *Spiritual empowerment, personal/ human development and self-determination;*
- *Human dignity, social justice, equality, solidarity;*
- *The exploitation of cultural and socio-human resources from the community and social context.*

*Empowerment it is one of the fundamental aim of practice in humanistic social work, achieved mainly through re-humanization, re-spiritualization and re-enlightenment of the individual and community – starting from the idea that, in the most part, the social issues and situations of difficulty have as explanation a pronounced deficit of humanism, spirituality and culture in the people's personality or socio-human communities.*

*Malcolm Payne (2011) associate the concept of humanistic social work to fundamental human rights, personal and spiritual development, creativity, responsibility and social justice, identifying as the main theoretical and methodological sources/ models the humanistic and phenomenological thinking, philosophy of existence, existential-humanistic psychology/ psychotherapy, transpersonal psychology, social constructivism and microsociology.*

*So, a key concept and value of humanistic social work theory and methodology is human being. The professional-client interaction is actually an inter-human relationship between two or more beings, with personality and soul, and, the success of the intervention is crucial determined by its nature and quality and not just by the economic resources or the used technology.*

*Through the imposing of the concept-system "humanistic social work" it marks the transition into a new phase, where the humanistic orientation it enhances and enriches their actual presence in social work theory, practice and policy, and makes it more than an occasional association of terms - a system-concept, a strong and unitary theory, and a distinct theoretical and methodological paradigm/ way of social work and social welfare... ... ... ... ... ... .......................................*

*... ... ... ..............................*

*As is well known, in social and human sciences, the term humanist/ humanistic/ humanism was consecrated through many meanings. We hold mainly two:*

*1) regarding to the human condition, the idea of ancestral human unity and solidarity; the representation of person as ontological part of a community, of people with souls, mutual conditioned by the ontogenetic interpersonal interaction - theoretical-axiological sources of the social solidarity and concern/ care for each other;*

*2) regarding to the intrinsic resources and capacities of the individual, as person, of affirmation, self-actualization, self-determination, personal achievement and development; the representation of the person as me, personality, with the attribute of will and freedom, creativity, responsibility and dignity - the sources of personal and social change and empowerment of the individual and the community.*

*The first meaning is, with predilection, exploited and stated by philosophy, religion, transpersonal psychology and anthropology, while the second by humanistic and positive psychology, pedagogy, psychotherapy and humanistic sociology.*

*In agreement with the two established theoretical-axiological meanings and the humanistic orientation from social work generates two relatively distinct forms of humanistic social work, i.e. the solidarist-humanistic social work and the positive-humanistic social work.*

*The solidarist-humanistic form, supported, therefore, theoretically, methodologically and axiologically by philosophy, religion, transpersonal psychology and anthropology, is closer or even identical, to some extent, with traditional social work, prioritizing the care for the comfort and welfare of the helpless person, for relieving the suffering, through various forms of assistance, through solidarity, altruism, compassion, attachment, empathy and compathy, while, the positive-humanistic form is closer to critical social work, through the interest for changing, but not for changing the social system but through empowerment, through the exploitation and capitalization of the resources of personality and of the socio-human context (compathy), with the theoretical support of the humanistic psychology, psychotherapy, pedagogy and sociology (microsociology/ humanistic sociology).*

*Although, strictly analytic, seems somewhat opposite, in fact, the two forms, solidarist-humanistic social work and positive-humanistic social work, are "two faces of the same coin", two sides and dimensions of the same process, subsumed to an unitary theory and practice of the humanistic social work, within the larger theoretical-methodological framework of the social work field as a whole.*

*In fact, in the current practice, all forms and orientations of the social work are found combined in various proportions and manners, determined by the philosophy of approach, ideology and the social policy, by the specific of problems, the used methods and by the pursued objectives...........................*

*...............................................................*

*Human suffering, unhappiness, personal failure, loss, dehumanization of the individual an community, emotional drama and great collective tragedies, disasters with significant human impact, personal/ community underdevelopment are among the central phenomena and categories of, what might be called, in scientific terms, the object of humanistic social work practice.*

*The human suffering, unhappiness, personal failure, loss, dehumanization of the individual are often related to a social problem, to a difficult situation, and, often, the normalization cannot be achieved without its elimination or limitation. Object of the humanistic social work it is also the lack of personal fulfillment, existential issues, personal and collective tragedies, etc.*

*Practitioners, in their daily professional activity, interact with unmet, professional or personal, individuals, who have failed or have deviated from the optimal way to achieve the personal, professional and social goals, who daily live chronic dissatisfaction and personal dramas.*

*Loss, separation, uprooting, loneliness, poverty, promiscuity, discrimination, marginalization are issues with great personal and social impact, but are also ontological or human problems. Each of these can be considered part of what, we might call, the phenomenon or process of dehumanization, human degradation of the individuals and communities.*

*The communities where predominate the undeveloped (human/ personal/ moral) individuals, selfish, individualistic, concerned only of the personal benefit are aprioristic prone to problems.*

*In humanistic paradigm of social work the vulnerability, difficult situation of the person is associated, mainly, with delays and disorders of personal and human development, with ontological inconsistency and poor quality of the interpersonal relations, with degradation of the values system (moral, cultural, etc.) of the community and organizations.*

*Any social group, community or organization is and an empathetic community. Many human suffering, tragedy or social problems are rooted in its underdevelopment, in weaknesses or very serious compathetic problems. The knowledge of this aspect by the social workers is a necessity and, moreover, the compathy, empathetic community, the system of sympathies and empathies can be very effective tools for change, improvement, normalization.*

*The empathetic community and compathy are build and specifically define through the common circumstances, characteristics and behaviors of individuals which compose it. Consists mainly of three types of processes or phenomena: emotional, cognitive and spiritual. In this perspective each member of a community is a product of a unique interaction, depending on the personality of others, place, time, cultural niche, hazard. Each person is actually part of a particular compathetic system. It is, in turn, part of a comprehensive system. The most common compathetic system and most consistent is the family... ... ... ... ... ... ... ... ... ... ... ... ... ... ... ....*

*... ... ... ... ... ... ... ... ... ... ... ... ...*

# Appendix 2

# "HUMANISTIC SOCIAL WORK PRACTICE"

*Operating into the sphere of social, human relationships, the main purpose of the humanistic social work practice is that to transform them in* **humane** *relationships, starting from the idea that the suffering, unhappiness, personal failure, loss, dehumanization of the individual an community have, largely, the main sources in the precariousness social and human relationships.*

*In this way reaching so to determine changes not at the society level, such as the critical/ radical social work, where it is the mission of the politician, nor at the body level, where it is the mission of the healthcare professional, but at the human, socio-human level, at the human relationships level, where it is its mission.*

*In this mission the humanistic practitioner is involved with whole its self, soul, intellect and experience, in the complex assembly of relations, connections, conflicts, attachments, inter-empathies, compathies, feelings, passions, loves, projects, dramas of the group with problems, he detect the dysfunctions, problems, under-developments, anomalies, building the diagnostic panel by an etiology and phenomenology of existential-humanistic type, focusing, therefore, on highlighting the dysfunctions from the human relations level, the intervention aiming, so, to convert them, by means of its knowledge, experiences, humane personality, soul, and psychological-spiritual qualities, as curative resources, in humane relationships.*

*The change for better from the human relations level, transformed into humane relations, will generate improvements, impressive qualitative changes at the micro-community level as a whole, as well at the level of each person; the transformative process evolving in cascade, involving humanizing sub-processes at all levels, eliminating many dysfunctions, disorders, problems, sufferings; the new created environment being defined by qualifiers such as spiritual and humane welfare, efficiency, socio-humane cohesion, harmony, solidarity, mutual aid, compathy, responsible, cooperation, humanity.*

*This environment will impose, ultimately, as a curative solution for many problems and difficult situations, and only to the extent that the professionals and social services manage to lead, generate it, with their activities, measures,* conducts can sustain that they operates thoroughly and efficiently, and meet their specific mission, at least in the perspective of the humanistic social work theory and axiology.

...................................................

.........................

Between the crucial values of the humanistic social work practice are social justice; personal and human development of the customers: the complexity of the client's personality, and of the client system; methodological flexibility; evidence-based practice; valorization of the client's creativity, freedom and resources; development of the self, and the capitalization of spiritual potential; the priority of the client's interests, feelings and values; spiritual well-being and development of the client and community; human development, empowerment and self-determination of the person / client and community; equality, solidarity, compathy; human relationships as humane relationships; the importance of the professional's personality, education, human qualities, conducts, value and principles in practice.

...................................................

...............................

Accountability, achieving personal and social equality, flexibility in human life and professional practice, complexity in human life and professional practice, achieving caring and creativity, developing self and spirituality, developing security and resilience, developments in research are, according to Payne (2011), the most important principles and values of the humanistic social work practice.

The main role of the humanistic social work practice is to enable the clients to realize their potential within the therapeutic relationship and socio-human context, by enhancing the client's potential, to achieve the self-actualization in social environment, also to create just social conditions to promote general well-being, to promote human and social well-being by developing the human capacities, social justice, equality, freedom, and mutual responsibility through shared social experience (Payne, 2011, p. 31).

..............................................

...............................

What would particularizes a code of ethics of the humanist social work practice in report to critical and/ or radical social work for example, which emphasizes the importance of the systems and structures generators of problems, inequality, suffering, social injustice, is the emphasis put, in the work of the services and professionals, on the exploitation of the resources of the personalities and socio-human contexts involved in the processes of assessment and intervention.

This aspect involves a huge responsibility of the services and professionals which one cannot invoke the system and structures for the failure of activity, and require from them very much engagement, responsibility, ethics, knowledge, skills, and professional relationships marked themselves of more humanism.

In humanistic social work "system" every professional has an active role in the promotion, development and advancement of all integrated social policies aimed at fostering social and civic advancement, emancipation and responsibility *within the community, and in any programs designed to improve the quality of life.*

*Also, the professional must deal with his colleagues, and any other professionals, with whom he is working, in a manner that is honest, polite, loyal and in a spirit of collaboration.*

..................................................

..................................

*The evidence-based practices and methods, in humanistic social work practice, propose, in the specific activity of evaluation, intervention and change, in casework, caring and therapy, etc., the focusing on the complex, phenomenological reality of the client by scientific knowledge, experimental research and methodical embedding of the previous clinical experiences.*

*So, in humanistic social work practice the practitioners can/ must embody flexible, contextual, but also knowledge-based responses to the complexities of the human personality and community, to the complexity of the situations of difficulty of the clients (Payne, 2011).*

*In this sense, the evidence-based practices involves, in the specific activity of the practitioner, of assessment and intervention, the focusing, both contextual/ existential and scientific, on the complex, phenomenological reality of the client.*

*The construction of the evaluative picture of system client starts, yet, with what is identified as existing, real, verifiable and sensitive (Payne, 2011: 76). Further, the practitioner's work is based on the evidence of researches and studies's conclusions on that type of case it works. This having the task to realize "modelings" of the identified difficult situations in report of the research's findings, without abdicating, but, from the fundamental values and principles of the humanistic social work related to the immense complexity of the socio-human phenomena and of the situations of difficulty in which are involved the clients.*

..................................................

..................................

*In the activities of identification, evaluation, diagnosis, design, planning, intervention, monitoring, in the objectives of psychological and social rehabilitation, the humanistic case management imply the focus on the human, spiritual, ontological, subjective issues of the client, of his life and difficult situation, on the concrete socio-human relationships and behaviors, where there is also the sources of evaluation and the resources of change/ rehabilitation.*

*The reason is that the vulnerability and the situation of difficulty, in humanistic social work practice, are accentuated by the psychosocial disengagement and human degradation which has suffered the client, the degradation of the interpersonal relationships, of the the concrete socio-human environment from the community (Horner, Kindred, 1997).*

*The humanistic case manager will build the evaluative table especially through a humanistic-spiritual phenomenology. The process of developing the project of intervention, after the humanistic model, involves giving priority to identify the spiritual, human, subjective, volitional needs and resources for rehabilitation/ change.*

It is envisaged as the used activities of intervention to not do excess of formalism and technicism, the professional must to empathize authentically with the client, following, principally, to contribute to her psychological and social empowerment through the spiritual, personal/ psychological, moral and socio-cultural development, through the valorization of his skills and creative abilities, including through work, economic, productive activity.

The institutions and the social services, in working on the cases, are not intended, usually, intimate objectives, related to the quality of the client's feelings, still they should to propose improvements also in regards the psychological life, otherwise the efforts could become useless. The solving of the social problem without concern towards the feelings and emotions of the clients, especially of the children, is a solving actually improper of the case.

Therefore, in humanistic social work practice, in case management and casework, in the humanistic process of intervention the emphasis will be placed on the involvement and exploitation of the spiritual, human, subjective, voluntary resources for rehabilitation of the client. The specific objectives of the activity include especially terms such as authentic happiness, personal development, accountability, social recovery/ integration through human, spiritual and moral development, the formation of a solid organizational culture, etc.

So, in humanistic casework must be outlined the importance and significant weight they have the subjective existence and spiritual life of the client, the feelings, values, self-esteem, personality in his private and social life to justify the necessity of prioritizing them in the hierarchy/ inventory of the clients's needs, and their transformation in assistential/ therapeutic resources and objectives (Reamer, 1993).

For the children from social institutions, for example, the personality (soul) is not only an ontological-psychological formation which must be cared but it is even objective of growth and education. Its healthy and functional formation is related to the objectives which are established relative to the hierarchy of needs. If on the foreground will be placed the interest of satisfying the basic needs, neglecting the socio-emotional, spiritual, personal, ontological-human needs then we should not wonder for the fact that the majority of the institutionalized children have great difficulty to integrate socially and are always sad, alienated, unhappy (Stefaroi, 2008, p. 68).

...................................................

..............................

The theory and axiology of the humanistic social work promotes the placement of the person separated from the natural family, especially of the children, until the eventual family reintegration and social integration, as optimal alternative to the placement in institutions, the placement in substitutive families, in extended family, neighbors, adoption, even if and here may occur many problems of human, ethical, social, psychological order.

.............................................................

...............................

As is well known in the wide system of social welfare and social work services many professionals performing activities with therapeutic character, whether we are talking actually of psychotherapists that treats the clients from the *institutions and services of social assistance of mental and behavioral disease related to the social problem as anxiety disorders, depressions, personality disorders, effects of sexual and physical abuse, of substance abuse, grief and bereavement, eating disorders, and others, either we talk of practitioners, of different professions, that address problems and deficiencies of language, motricity and psychomotricity, social, etc., provided to children, people with disabilities, addicts, elderly, unemployed, to individuals or communities (families, organizations etc.).*

*A large group of professionals that perform activities with therapeutic character in the wide system of social welfare and social work services is represented by the social workers with specific training, certified and with right of free practice, well known also as clinical social workers, some are called even simple therapists, but focused on the psycho-behavioral problems of the clients of the services of social assistance.*

*As is normal the followers of the humanistic psiho-therapeutical guidelines use the well known modalities and methods of the humanistic psychotherapy practice, adapting them, of course, to the specific problematic and casuistry of the services of social work, the main purpose is, in this respect, to rehabilitate, socially and humanly, the client, even if for the practitioner must operate interventions in the psychological or somatic sphere.*

*Thus, among the most important psychotherapeutic methods and ways is distinguished the client/person-centered methods, the existential methods, the gestalt methods, the positive methods and appreciative methods, the balance method, etc.*

*Essentially, these therapeutic modalities of intervention, rehabilitation, change and empowering promotes the peer relationship between the therapist and the client, focusing on the client's needs and feelings, through his human and spiritual development and empowerment, To this end the therapist/ clinical social worker can use the internal experiences of the clients as core resources.*

*The main concentration is on the client's self-determination, the development of his self-control and the will and determination to change his condition through spiritual, moral, human, personal development.*

*In this end the psychological and personological qualities such as empathy and compathy, spiritual welfare and virtue, happiness and eudaimonic-altruistic energy/ motivation, personal development, humane development and humanity, the humane, prosocial and charismatic, compathetic behavior of the professional being very important.*

*The reason is that in the therapeutical process between the practitioner's personality and the client's personality being established a high psychological-ontological interconnection, congruence (emotional, empathetic, humane, spiritual). In this sense we can states the truth the professional's humane personality should be considered one the main resource of the humanistic therapist or humanistic clinical social worker, both when we pursue the psychological-eudaimonical objectives or the integrative, prosocial objectives.*

# Appendix 3

## " HUMANISTIC SOCIAL WORK:

## *Personality and Human Relations*
## *– Basic Resources of Practice"*

*Humanistic social work, as theory and practice, is based on an ensemble of theories and methods largely having its origins in humanistic psychotherapy, but adapted to the specific of activity from social work areas, ie the solving of socio-human and collective problems and not only individually problems (Payne, 2012).*

*Regardless of the specific and nature of the object of intervention humanistic social work use this unlimited and miraculous resources: the human personality (being) and the human (humane) relations. This is the reason why its theory and methodology operates with concepts like human being, soul, person, self, empathy, compathy, personal development, spirituality, culture, socio-human context, microcommunity, solidarity etc., especially when aims objectives at the family, organizational or community level.*

*Therefore, the epistemological and methodological foundation of humanistic social work is, ultimately, the representation of individual client as personality, soul, being, and moving in the background the representation as body or through elementary social relationships, as well as the representation of the collective client as a compathetic interaction between persons with soul, personality, as human beings, also as a complex systems of human relations, represented mainly as humane relationships.*

*To this end, the practitioners, through traits like humane qualities, high empathetic quality/ capacity, through creativity, aesthetic sensibility, authentic faith, happiness and eudemonic energy/ motivation, concern for truth, balanced personality, through spirituality and humanness will send and stimulate the development of the humane, spiritual and eudemonic features at the customers level too, factually sending positive energy, happiness, aesthetic, intellectual, spiritual, playful qualities; thus contributing, to a greater extent, on their personal and human development, increasing the self-esteem, social consciousness, the capacity of initiative and social autonomy. Thus fulfilling the true mission of the humanistic social work practice.*

*So, humanistic social work prioritizes and promotes the human personality as resource and operates with an empathetic professional personality concept, that combines the humane personality with pragmatic personality. Therefore, in the staff training process the focus is on humanistic curriculum, the goal is to train and cultivate the humane, empathetic professional personality, the capacity to resonate to the customers' sufferings and problems.*

*Qualities such as empathy, presence of spirit, high level of general culture, aesthetic sensibility, faith and respect for the moral/ religious values, playfulness, communicativity should not miss to any social worker or a psychologist, or a caregiver, because it is the concrete person that empathizes with the customer. So, the humanist worker in social welfare practices is not concerned only of the customer survival, but aims the human development, rehabilitation in perspective, according to a human "project", building a new modus vivendi and a new architecture of personality. Without vision, without idealization, without projectivity his personality remains contingent, flat, obtuse. The humanistic goals will remain only on the paper. All what aims to build at the client level must exist first in his personality, in its onto-ideational/ projective interior universe. The projectivity, vision, hope are both the professional qualities and the main resources and means to achieve the objectives of humanistic social work practice. These are inherent dimensions of personality and human condition, but must be cultivated and educated.*

*Here, we see, the fundamental role is of the general educational system, but also of the system of training the personnel for social work areas. When in the domain of social work will work mostly people with above characteristics are probable to decline, gradually, the number of assisted persons and the situation of those from the system becoming better. Yet, the idea that seems to impose is that the solid, lasting, efficiency personal development and client empowerment is also conditioned by the organizational and cultural level of the community where he lives or by the quality of human and interpersonal relationships in group. (Bradford and Burke, 2005).................*

...........................................................................................

*In accordance with the principles of humanistic psychology each healthy individual has the potential capacity to fulfill as person, to be happy, in human, social and spiritual terms, but everything depends of its internal activism, of willingness to self-change or accomplishment, but, also, and of the identification and use the resources, including with the professional aid (Rogers, 2008).*

*The humanistic theories represent the client as being itself, as soul, subject of silent suffering and happiness, and not only as a neutral individual of a social system, or humble beneficiaries of the community services. Humanistic theories convert the client from individual to person, to human being, to I, in subject, to soul.*

*The humanist-spiritual perspective on customer promotes the taking into account its aesthetic, playful, epistemological and mystical needs. Namely, the spiritual needs. Meeting and development the spiritual needs, the development of the spiritual personality is one of the most effective methods/ ways for the personal development of customer, and enhance the perspective of personal/ social empowerment, regardless of the education level, origin, age or types of social/ human problems.*

*Humanistic social work, the third way in social work, takes over from traditional social work the care for the client as person, being, soul, personality and focus on the socio-human, compathetic, concrete context/ environment where he lives, while, from the critical/ radical social work the interest for social/ human progress and change. In the first case humanistic social work operates mainly with the concept of empathy, while in the second with the concept of empowerment. The two terms, empathy and empowerment, having a constitutional role in the practice of humanistic social work.*

*In this perspective the mission of humanistic social work practice would be to promote a compathetic attitude in the practitioner-client relationship, by creating a complex system of humane relations, a socio-human environment based on empathy, love and humanity, by humanizing the community, by changing the customers and communities through empowerment, personal/ community development and responsibility, starting from the person/ community right to happiness and well-being, but also from their right to dignity and self-determination.*

*One of the most important mission of the humanistic social work practice is the interventions in the personal and social crises, dramatic or at limit situations. The professionals from social work services are faced and with social and human problems caused by political or economic crises, social, natural or health disasters, blows, with great economical, psychological or medical impact. Some of these cannot be overcome because of the force of impact, damaging, irreparably, destinies, lives, careers, families, communities.*

*The affected people and communities experiences individual or collective dramas, impossible to describe, which the workers from social services must to intuit the human dimension, to represent them at the true intensity and meaning, to be helpful and to intervene through the humanistic social work methods, to improve the situations, relief of suffering and mitigate the effects, especially on children... ... ... ... ... ... ... ... ... ... ... ... ... ...*

*... ... ... ... ... ... ... ...*

*Decrease the pain of unhappy customer, growth the spiritual well-being, personal development and gaining autonomy through empowerment, personal/ social/ moral/ spiritual development and social-human integration are among the most important tasks of the humanistic practitioner.*

*In the complex and unitary methodological context the humanistic practitioner will focus especially on the spiritual, psychological and socio-human sphere of the client's personality. The goal is and the ontological harmonization of internal and external relationships within the group/ community, with effects on the development of the personality's ontological consistency of the person/ client and diminishing the risk to entry in risk or difficult situation.*

*So, one of the most important role of the humanistic social worker is to enable the client, a person or community, to become capable of coping with the crisis situations and difficult situations which can appears any time.*

*This must to promote, also, the social justice, personal development of the customers, the complexity of human being, methodological flexibility, the capitalization of the client's creativity, development of the Self and the capitalization of spiritual potential of the human personality. The humanistic social worker have also a consistent role of educator, trainer, which involves mainly giving information and developing skills to clients, but first, must be a good educator, must to be himself knowledgeable and a good communicator.*

*Because, in humanistic social work practice, between the practitioner's personality and the client's personality is established a high degree of congruence, (empathetic, human, spiritual) the cultivation of spiritual and human values of the professional personality, as well as the achievement of a consistent specific literature is an important theoretical concern.*

*The practitioner in humanistic social work takes from traditional social work qualities like sensitivity, caring for the other, altruism and from radical and critical social work the determination and ability to change the people. In humanistic social work this qualities are found, at the humanistic practitioner, mainly as capacity of empathy/ compathy and capacity to change through empowerment.*

*Humanistic social work, so the third way and new concept, theory and practice in contemporary social work, proposes a new concept and approach of the practitioner and his personal qualities, personality traits. It is a prioritize of the human and spiritual qualities, certainly not disregard other types of qualities. Features such as human sensitivity, soulful/ spiritual well-being and personal happiness, agreeableness, spiritual sensitivity, vocation for working with the suffering person, balanced personality, vision and projectivity, tolerance, anti-discrimination, idealism are increasingly required by employers from social work agencies, and are increasingly taken into consideration in the activity of training the staff.................*

*.............................................................................*

*Human and spiritual qualities of the practitioner have as the most important source, the human personality, especially the soul. The mere existence, as the ontological core of personality, of the soul determines the empathy, compassion, love, aesthetic sensitivity, attachment, conception of the world, religious faith, the human sensitivity. Concrete form of expression and intensity depending, of course, of the stage of development or of many others individual characteristics.*

*In the process of personality formation, by establishing the soul, it occurs the humanization of the body, animation through the other (generic man, the source), the one who must be assimilated, so that, the body from birth to become a man. In its absence the body would become what cybernetics try to build, with the intention of imitating the human beings, a robot.*

*The formation and establishment of the soul causes the body to become a human and not a robot, therefore it is so important to raising the children in families, in environments based on attachment, affection, respect for each other. The other one is the source of their development.*

*There is a common spiritual background, which incorporate the relational-affective pattern of the human being, the structure of personal background that determines the overall empathetic capacity and the human sensitivity, but there is and a specialization according to the particular psychological characteristics, or of social/ professional environment, which favors the attachment. The soulful configuration of an artist is generally different from that of a butcher. As well, the configuration and soulful/ empathetic quality of a social worker is different from that of an engineer.*

*In this end, humanistic social work theory and practice operates with an empathetic professional personality concept, that combines the humane personality with pragmatic personality. Therefore, in the practitioners training process the focus is on humanistic curriculum, the goal is to training and cultivation the empathetic-professional personality, the ability to resonate to the sufferings and problems of the customers.*

*Qualities such as empathy, presence of spirit, the high level of general culture, aesthetic sensibility, faith and respect for the moral/ religious values, playfulness, communicativity and openness should not miss to any social worker or a psychologist, or a caregiver, because this is, in the process of evaluation or intervention, the concrete person wherewith empathize the customer.*

*As well the personality formation is also a process of spiritualization and the training of the professional human personality is primarily a process of spiritualization and humanization.*

*In the general process of personalization by the spiritual personality appearance, as onto-formation, also and of the soul, is made a subtle, sublime and complex process of spiritualization, with essential influence, by feedback, on self-personality, social personality and social life.*

*The effect is that the individual make the jump from the psychic and personality at the person and from the animal at the human, in the anthropological and cultural definition. The spiritualization involves the separation (relative) from the nature, from raw material and anchoring on the magical ideas world, in the playful and aesthetic metaphor. Requires the capitalization of the inexhaustible resources offered by the historical human creation, by culture and religion. Offers to the human, in general, and to the professional personality, in particular, the capacities and personal qualities like empathy, altruism, spiritual sensibility, soulfulness, happiness, humanism, etc.*

*Through human, empathetic capacity, through creativity, aesthetic sensibility, authentic faith, concern for truth, balanced personality the professionals will send and stimulate the development of spiritual features to the customers too, factually sending positive energy, happiness, aesthetic, intellectual, spiritual, playful qualities; thus contributing to a greater extent of their personal development, increase self-esteem, social consciousness, the capacity of initiative and social autonomy. Thus fulfilling the true mission for the humanistic social work practice: empowerment, social inclusion and happiness.*

*The objective of practice, focused on person, would be to stimulate the development or formation of a personality structure where the spiritual formation is consistent and has high percentage in the structure and economy of personality - the client will have an optimistic but realistic self perception, a relatively high self-esteem, confidence, aspirations, an consistent ego. Also, it will be describe like an active, adaptive person, with functional interpersonal relationships, presence of spirit, eager for social reintegration and regain dignity.*

*Empathy is, without doubt, one of the underused therapeutic resources in social science and practices (Rogers, 1959), including social work. But the humanistic social work pay it a crucial role. Empathy and compathy are phenomena and processes of great complexity, depth and finesse, that involve, concurrent, the subject and the other, the person and the group, the individual and the society, the group and society, values and beliefs, feelings and ideas, the material and spiritual existence.*

*The study of the empathetic phenomena and processes, the empathy as object of scientific knowledge is not only a epistemological necessity but also a necessity of higher social and human importance in the globalization perspective, the effects of "cybernetisation" and "virtualization" of the social life, the moral and cultural degradation, degradation of the family values, growth of the economic-technical factor role in society and in the daily life of the humans.*

*About the psychosocial concept and phenomenon that is empathy have dealt great thinkers, like Lipps (to feel something in himself), Allport (understanding and feeling each other), Titchener (ability to think and feel what another person thinks and feels), Rogers (the fourth stage in the emotional-personal development; ability to really sit in the other's place, of seeing the world as he sees it), Batson (disposition/ motivation oriented to the other).*

*Hoffman (2000) interprets the empathic disposition of the person as effect of cognitive-affective action of the other, resulting so an emotional response closer to the other interests than the self. Other authors gives the following meanings to the concept of empathy: sympathetic projection of the self, emotional fusion, sympathetic intuition, affective union, knowledge by interweaving, introjection, tranzitivism, intropathy, sympathy, transposition into the current other's state, identification with another, transfer, sympathetic projection.*

*Empathy is a form of knowledge of the environment, so is a cognitive process, is a form of feeling and emotional experience to the other, therefore, is an emotional process, is an interpersonal process, so is a social process and, not least, is a spiritual process/ phenomenon, through the human capacity to resonate to the culture, science, philosophy, religion, etc. All these phenomena and processes contribute to the establishment of what might call the humane sensitivity.*

*Any social group, community or organization is and an empathetic community. Many human suffering or social problems are rooted in its underdevelopment, in weaknesses or serious compathetic problems. Knowledge of this aspect by the humanistic professionals is a necessity and, moreover, the compathy, empathetic community, the system of sympathies, empathies, transpathies can be very effective tools for change, improvement, normalization of the client/ community.*

*Each member of a community is a product of a unique interaction, depending on the personality of the others, place, time, cultural niche, hazard. Each person is actually part of a particular compathetic system. It is, in turn, part of a comprehensive system. The most common compathetic system and most consistent is the family.*

*The compathetic consistency is given by the fact that the individual personalities are composed of shared experiences, by the fact that in each individual personality exists, through empathy and projection, the others. Establish a mutual existential dependence.*

*This empathetic community works, through the organizational culture, and as a system of symbols or values that are rooted in the individual's personality or activism. These symbols and values it imposes as link and unity resort between the two parties. Their existence and operation gives the sense of belonging, familiar, known, give comfort, safety and happiness.*

*Between the empathetic community and individuals which it constitute it establish a socio-ontological balance, an existential and functional optimum, in which it is satisfy, in principle, an harmonious and non-confrontational way, both the personal and collective necessities.*

*Empathetic community and compathy can also have and negative influences, may be an area of non-value, of conflict, hostility or social exclusion. The empathetic community can have a coherent organization and functioning but founded on non-value, on antisocial attitudes, or may be poorly organized, dysfunctional, immature. In both cases, members are exposed to personal underdevelopment, marginalization and social/ moral maladjustment.*

*The empathetic capacity and behavior is not an alternative but a consubstantial necessity of any profession on the social work field, especially in the child welfare/ social work, but and in the elderly and disabled. Through empathy their personality becomes sensitive to the sufferings and problems to people in need, and, at the behavioral level, acquires agreeability.*

*Through empathetic qualities, namely, the ability to feel the enjoyment (desire, suffering) of the other, the ability to think and experience what another person thinks and feels, the ability to really put in the another place, to see the world as he/ she sees, the personal provision/ motivation to the other, sympathetic projection of the self, emotional-affective fusion, sympathetic intuition, introjection, transitivism, intropathy, sympathy, identification with the other, transfer etc. the professional acquires access to the customer's personality and an effective method of therapeutic change. The empathy of practitioner operates through its defining functions: cognitive, of communication and foresight, of emotional contagion and performance, of solidarity, pro-social etc.*

*It is a fundamental way to knowing the customer and the environment where he lives, so, a cognitive process, is a form of feeling and emotional reflection of the client/ environment, therefore, is an emotional process; being and a interpersonal process is and a social process, and, not least, a spiritual process/ phenomenon through the capacity of the practitioner's personality to resonate at the customer's culture and spiritual sensitivity.*

*The empathetic qualities of the professional in an institution for residential care are of great importance in the goal to achieve the organizational congruence, consistency, unity and functionality. In these institutions, the empathy must have a very important role. The professional-client inter-empathy has an undeniable curative function (Rogers, 1959).*

*Care institution is a network of inter-empathy that, especially in children's institutions, the professional's personality can have a vital educational function. The professional's personality interacts with all its physical, psychological, social, cultural, moral level and features:personal characteristics - age, appearance, personality etc.; language; specific sensory-cognitive and affective qualities; system of values, sensibilities, tastes, habits, rules, customs, etc.;behaviors, gestures, activities, etc.*

*The organization/ institution of social care it is defined and by the personalities that made up, including the personalities of professionals, with the three dimensions: socio-affective, cognitive and spiritual. The affective phenomena are in fact, relationships, interactions, compathies between the affective spheres of the persons, while the cognitive and spiritual phenomena are the processes between its spiritual spheres or projective egos.*

*Through the spiritual and social valences of the empathetic personality a practitioner from a residential institution for children can help to create a magical psychosocial and cultural "universe" for the satisfaction of intimate, deep, empathetic personal needs, of spiritual growth and education, emotional and moral development of the children. The institution is for the child the place where is built the ontological foundations of its personality. Is the environment where the child is feed with spiritual and moral energy. Is the existential magic framework of training, existence and manifestation of his personality, of its happiness and soulful/ personal fulfillment.*

*The happiness theme is approached from all possible perspectives: philosophical, psychological, religious, anthropological, aesthetic, sociological etc. The dominant idea, which seems to be clear is that the happiness is not directly determined by the current, libidinal, sensorial pleasure and satisfaction, but rather of a deep, constitutional/spiritual personality structure, which also predisposes the person to personal development, social efficiency, positive emotions and feelings.*

*This is also the basic assumption of the book "Authentic Happiness" by Martin Seligman (2002. After Seligman the authentic happiness is conditioned by the optimal development at the all motivation levels of the personality: hedonic, of the desires, of the ego and of the objectives. Another author, Jonathan Haidt, addressing the theme of happiness in the book "The Happiness Hypothesis" (2006), through the concept of metaphor.*

*Happiness is usually perceived as being related to achieving personal fulfillment, so they are at the higher level of the motivational pyramid and structure of personality. Is identified also with positive, euphoric feelings, with the satisfaction or pleasure, states that can be related to the needs from the lower levels. No doubt, elements and dimensions of the happiness (the need for happiness) can be found at all levels of the human personality.*

*For the social welfare system we believe that the most appropriate sense of happiness would be her description in terms of unitary structure and functioning of the personality, with the states of equilibrium and efficiency that they generates. In this context we say that the need of happiness is in fact the need of psychological balance, of balanced personal structure, adaptable personality, personal development in the physical, psychological, spiritual and social plan.*

*In the happiness theory in social work's perspective (Stefaroi, 2009b) a person is, or becomes a client of social services not only because of the social or economic circumstances, as is often stated, but because his personality is socio-maladaptive structured, and an essential role in this process it has the unmet or vicious meet of the need of happiness, of positive mental states, of satisfaction, of supply the ego, self-esteem. In vain is intervenes on the individual client system with economic or social measures if the problem has, in fact, an important psychological, emotional, or psychological-spiritual component.*

*In humanistic social work the relation with the client is not objectual but human, "spiritual". The term can help us to understand more deeply, completely and complex the nature and specific of the professional-customer relationship. Beyond the primary goal of the social reintegration or economic rehabilitation, the customer expects also related services such as tolerance, understanding, humor, aesthetics sensibility, morality, creativity, "spirituality" (Stefaroi, 2009b, p.174).*

*The recruitment activity of the professionals is intended so that the future employees to have the qualities that enable it to offer and such "services", to which often depends the success of the intervention. These are key determinants of the professional's efficiency in social work. Authentic source of these qualities is the soul and the established happiness state, the existence of a well developed onto-formations of happiness and a positive hedonic-affective onto-balance.*

*It is impossible to imagine professional efficiency, in the jobs that involve working with people, without human-personal efficiency, with the soulful welfare and happiness state which it implies. Literature concludes that the professionalism is strongly conditioned by the degree of happiness and interior comfort of the person. The professional efficiency is correlated with the positive attitudes, with the degree of internal relaxation, the irony and personal happiness (Bandura, 1986). James (1981) believes that the job happiness/ satisfaction is, in fact, the relationship between the individual aspirations and the achievements. At the same time, happiness is an onto-subjective psychological feature and it aprioristic makes the professionals to performance.*

*We believe that the following psychological-soulful/ human/ spiritual predispositions promote the efficiency of the professional in humanistic social work practice, in the effort to adapt and achieve the specific professional tasks: soulful welfare, state of happiness, self-esteem, functional flexibility, agreeability, extraversion, democratic spirit, tolerance, openness to new ideas, epistemological and methodological flexibility, mature personality, emotional stability, self-control, detachment, and, very important, the projectivity.*

*In the ontological order of the person/ personality projectivity gives the defining note as human being through the ontification of the generalized/ idealized other ("pattern" of the human beings), the values, ideas, knowledge, ideals, hopes. In fact, it's an interior ontic universe, which summarizes, through double onto-projection, the subjective and the objective, the body and the environment, the inside and the outside, the feeling and the thinking.*

*The onto-projective formation not emerge directly from the basic needs and psychological foundations of the person, like the hedonic ontos, phobic formation or the ontical subject, these arising at random from the particular dynamics of the relationship with the socio-human and cultural environment, reflecting, in a transformative/ projective way, its features. The objects, people, situations are not assimilation in their physical-sensorial objectuality but through the social/ cultural meanings, onto-projective idealized and subjectivated.After being constituted the onto-projective formations operates like some mechanisms in the subject and the other's service, through the projection of the endemic needs, individual desires and values, but and in the service of the other (environment, values, people) which "project", "inject" the vectors of control in person's formations, especially through education/ culture. In this way the individual's behaviors are doubled, guided, the individual is placed in a position to make difficult choices, compromises.*

*Onto-projective formations are, in fact, targets, hedonic-projective ideals, desires, aspirations which guide the conscious and unconscious searches/ choices for the ontogenetical-personal growth, training and development. These tend to holistically curdle in what we might call the project (print) of the personal training and development, i.e. the ideal of the good and personal happiness, the idealized image of the good and of the individual happiness.Operates, experiential and emergent, by complex mechanisms of feed-back and feed-before, through the onto-projective personal referents. The projective personal referents may be the desirable social status, the personal welfare, the desirable body image, the desirable profession, the required level of intelligence and knowledge, the aspirated physical and spiritual pleasures, the aesthetic, moral, axiological aspirations, etc. (for the social services, especially those dealing with children, some of them are actually educational and welfare objectives).*

*The perspectives in favor of its meeting installs positive emotions and states, comforting feelings, happiness. Instead, the low perspective of identifying with this hypostasis determines uncomfortable neurovegetative react and depression. The predominance of positive onto-projective feelings will lead to the establishment of a strong onto-formation of happiness and a visionary personality, tilting the balance in the positive side. So, through fixings the projective-personal balance in a favorable inclination will orient the personality to the future, will give it a positive sense, pleasant, efficient, active, dynamic, adaptable.*

*Projectivity, visionary and idealism are indispensable qualities of the professional in social work, because represents one of the most important onto-psychological source of the empathy, but, also, because the professions from social work are is teleological by its nature and mission. The humanistic professional from social work practice do not make only care, do not concerned only to the customer survival, but aims the human development, rehabilitation in perspective, according to a human "project"; by building, so, a new modus vivendi and a new architecture of the personality. Without vision, without idealization, without projectivity his personality remains contingent, flat, obtuse. The humanistic goals will remain only on paper. All that aims to build at the professional level must to exist in his personality, in its onto-ideational/ projective interior universe.*

*The customer's rehabilitation, development and happiness can be best achieved by operating on the projective onto-referents of the onto-projective sphere. But these must be, primarily, present at the practitioner's personality level. Therefore, in education and training of the professionals is important to put great emphasis on the training and to the eudemonic/ axiological onto- referents, perceived with roles of anchors, ideals, human values.*

*The process leads to form a vigorous professional personality, human, active, positive, autonomous, oriented to self-achievement but and to the other's wellbeing. Also, the process develops psychic functions like the will, motivation, imagination, intelligence (including emotional). Projectivity, vision are both the professional qualities and the main resources and means of achieving the objectives of humanistic social work practice. These are, also, inherent dimensions of the personality and human condition, but must be cultivated and educated.*

*The assessment of the personality traits such as altruism, agreeability, tolerance, kindness and projectivity and not only of professional skills and knowledge is increasingly common practice in the recruitment and evaluation practice of practitioners in social care system. The reason is very simple - to work with people, especially in suffering, difficulties calls for these qualities. In the assessment process, therefore, are followed and personality traits such as the humanism, playful spirit, cheerfulness, good general appearance, sociability, agreeability, vocation for working with the person in distress, balanced personality, interior comfort, irony, flexibility, extroversion, tolerance, nondiscrimination, adaptability, respect for life, happiness and other personal values, idealism, confidence in the capabilities of the person/ client self-actualization and self-determination, emotional stability, self-control, presence of spirit, resistance to frustration, openness to new ideas and values, etc.*

*Conversely, the following devices, disposition and personality factors limit, hinders the worker's efficiency in the effort to achieve the professional duties, we mean to chronically psychological distress, lack of tolerance for irony, depression background, resistance to change, tendency to conserve a system of values and norms, opposition to new, conformism - obedience, lack of flexibility and suppleness of thought, dogmatism, reduced adaptability, stubbornness, misconceptions, unfounded ideas, attitudinal rigidity, resistance to information and change, to correction, inflexible attitudes to food, dress, political preference, sexual orientation, minorities, discrimination, emotional lability, immature personality, increased irritability, selfishness, lack of presence of spirit, etc.*

*Humanistic social work practice require from the practitioner a conduct concentrated to the human and soulful problems/ manifestations of the client. Through the humanistic knowledge and spiritual qualities in the assessment activity the humanistic professional it focuses on the identification, analysis and description the concrete customer's human problem and suffering, through the identification the situations of existential impasse or crisis, identification of the personal and collective tragedies, personal, family, organizational or professional failure situations.*

*Through humanistic methods it makes the representation of the current compathetic, social, cultural and psychosocial situations, of the concrete situations of depersonalization and dehumanization. Therefore, the humanistic practitioner will build the diagnosis mainly by a contextual-humanistic phenomenology. The process of construction the intervention plan after humanistic model involves the identification, primarily, of the soulful, spiritual, human, subjective, voluntary needs and resources of rehabilitation.*

*The intervention activities do not excess of formalism and technicism, the professional empathize authentically with the customer, aims to contributing to its social empowerment through the spiritual, personal/ psychological, moral and socio-cultural development (Payne, 2011). Through empathetic-projectiv behavior the professional working at the construction of a new interior/ soulful and exterior/ relational realities and behaviors of the clients, with humanistic tools. The behavior in the intervention process require increasing the role of the affective processes in therapeutic relationship, focusing on the customer's human and spiritual development, the intervention on resources and not on problems (Payne, 2011b), identifying the soulful/ existential anxieties/ crisis and internal-ontological re-equilibration through spiritual, human and moral development.*

*In the intervention process the targets mainly include terms such as human rehabilitation, authentic happiness, personal development, social recovery/ integration by spiritual and moral developing, formation of a strong organizational culture, accountability etc. The used methods aims, through the intervention plan, caring the soul and active personality. The humanistic social worker coordinating the team efforts to optimize the client's personality and the empathetic environment of the organization.*

*From the viewpoint of the humanistic values, principles and theories the training, recruitment and appraisal of the staff is a unitary phenomenon, and seeks, ultimately, as the workers to be not some mere servants who simply delivers some "services" but a complex human beings, with souls, with empathetic personality, with a deep knowledge of what is the human, like existence extremely complex. The professional, at the beginning of the Third Millennium, is able to contribute effectively both to reducing the client's suffering and to increase their ability to adapt and autonomous integrate in community. The formative-educational objectives are achieved mainly by promoting the humanistic values and model of the professional in social care areas, through the specific literature or through the educational system, by increasing the number of humanistic courses, of humanistic psychology, pedagogy and sociology, of philosophy, culture theory, anthropology.*

*This is because the humanistic practitioner is focused, with priority, on the soul, on the spiritual, empathetic, subjective, emotional issues of the client, on the existential bottlenecks, on group and personal dramas, on the moral and spiritual aspects of the problem. For it, the real problems are of human, emotional, spiritual nature.*

The humanistic counseling is a systematic approach, developed by professional tools and methods, in which an accredited counselor, providing assistance and support for spiritual/ human rehabilitation and socio-human adaptation.

And the manager or the worker from the residential institution, in the view of humanistic social work values, is a "man with a big soul". Human/ soulful qualities, the positive, compathetic, visionary personality prints the manager's behavior flexibility, adaptability, sociability, communication, agreeability, tolerance, it focuses on the human goals of the care institution, helps to prevent and resolve serious conflicts at all levels - intrapersonal, interpersonal, of group or institutional, enhances the complacency degree of customers and staff, of happiness, enhances the positive feeling of belonging to the organization.

It is essential that everyone who work in residential institutions to meet a minimum conditions of humane, educational, vocational, psychological or moral order. The organizations where they work must be themselves a source of stability, efficiency and humanism for the customers (Stefaroi, 2007). That is because the empathetic ability, emotional wellbeing, happiness, altruism, agreeability, intelligence, culture, idealism, visionary orients the workers through the achievement of humanistic goals of the care institution. The positive effects are felt over time particularly by shifting focus from the care of the body to the care of the soul and personality.

Thus, in humanistic social work practice the professional is interested, besides in material wealth, food, housing, comfort, also in spiritual wellbeing of the suffering person, in his dignity and condition as human being, with all rights implied by this existential statute.

The quality of human relationships, cultural quality of the community where lives the client, the quality of socio-moral climate are important factors that are part of the same concern for the soul and personality care and for enhance the perspectives of the humane rehabilitation and socio-human integration.

To this end, the practice is focused on the restoration/ improving the humane relationships in communities, using, especially methods and techniques like the intervention centred on the client's personality, and the intervention centred on humane relationships; personality and humane relationships being the most important resources of practice in humanistic social work – the third way in contemporary social work theory and method, alongside traditional social work and critical/ radical social work. ... ...............................................

# CONCLUSIVE CONSIDERATIONS

The HUMANISTIC SOCIAL WORK Project, the aegis under which this book, focused on the humane and spiritual qualities of the professional, is published has, firstly, the destignation to provide a formal framework for publishing works that have, especially, topics from the humanistic social work areas, and, so, to promotes the specific theory and methodology, but the process whereby the humanistic social work could, effectively, to acquire an own and consistent theory and methodology is not at all simple.

Humanistic social work, as well as other theoretical and practical areas who applied the label *humanistic,* has its limits and optimal application areas, quite narrowly defined, even, as happens in most cases when we operate with *isms*, tends to assign meanings of universality. Here it should be mentioned that the theories, methods and practices of the cognitive, behaviorist, psycho-dynamic, sociologist orientations still retains its usefulness, applicability, alongside the humanities, on the grounds that the multitude of theories and approaches reflects, in fact, the diversity and complexity of the social and human phenomena and processes, the complex, multicausal etiology of the social problems, the diversity of methods and effective practices used by the professionals and the social welfare services.

Undoubtedly, regarding the sphere of applicability, the theories, methods and practices of humanistic social work, we can speak of two perspectives. One would be that covering the entire system of social welfare, social work theory and practice, but focusing on aspects/ dimensions that involves a holistic humanistic approach and representtation, imposing a philosophical and methodological positioning in the context of connections with other types of approaches. The other perspective concerns a delimitation of areas, categories of problems and clients where the theories, methods and practices expressly humanistic should be indicated, more effective, more appropriate, such as family and child, older people, people suffering from trauma with major psychosocial impact, people with disabilities, children separated from parents, institutionalized persons, etc.

Regarding the "dispute" with the two major "modes" of social work/ welfare, respectively traditional social work and critical/ radical social work, here too, it can be stated that humanistic social work can easily find their place, and imposing as the third "mode" of social work/ welfare, or the third way, fact facilitated by the existence, since the establishment of social work/ welfare as current practice, more or less institutionalized/ nationalized, of the humanistic values and principles, and the presence, increasingly consistent, of the theories and methods originating in other areas of the humanistic theory and practice, mainly in humanistic psychology/ psychotherapy with subdomains such as client-centered psychotherapy, existential psychology/ psychotherapy, gestalt psychology/ psychotherapy, etc.

Trying a parallel with humanistic psychology, called the third way/ force in psychology, after, or alongside psychoanalysis and behaviorist psychology, it can be identified similarities with the positioning of the humanistic social work facing to traditional social work and critical/ radical social work, placing on the same side psychoanalysis with traditional social work, and in the other side the behaviorist psychology with critical/ radical social work.

Of course, the comparison and associations can seem forced, or circumstantial, but is, however, a fact, that psychoanalysis and traditional social work are important forms of onset of psychology and social assistance, both interested and focused on the body, emotions, with little interest in systemic or exterior determinism, such as, is real also the fact that the behaviorist psychology and critical/ radical social work emphasizes the role of the social system, environment, education, context in determining the problems and difficult situations of the clients, promoting, therefore, especially, methods that provide solutions from the outside of their subjectivity/ personality/ community.

Also regarding the professional's personality it is interesting to note the aspect that humanistic social work theory and axiology does not promotes a unilateral representation of the professional, of its qualities and conducts, even if, looked, for example, from the perspective of critical/ radical social work to humanistic approach it can reproach the exaggerated interest for spiritual and humane qualities, at the expense of scientific training and professional rigor.

In reality, humanistic social work, as suggests also the origins of the term *humanism*, in which to the knowledge are given a privileged role, closely linked to the idea of human rights, emancipation and affirmation, promotes the scientific training, and, in conclusion, multilateral and complex, of the professional; one of the reasons being the fact that only a complex, deep and accurate knowledge of the socio-human, economic, cultural and spiritual issues of the client can facilitate an effective entry in compathetic and eudemonic-curative congruence with the humane personality and resources, with the psychological-spiritual energies of the practitioner.

In this regard, the professional's personality, in the perspective of theory, axiology and methodology of humanistic social work, is a psychosocial and cultural construction of very high complexity, gathering, ontogenetically, the natural datum with education/ training, the internal resources with life and professional experience.

The professional's personality is, thus, metaphorically speaking, a huge reservoir of energy, knowledge, attitudes, feelings and habitudes with which the professional to work to achieve the two main goals of the practice: 1) empowerment, autonomization, rehabilitation and social integration, and  2) reduction the sufferings, soulful fulfillment, happiness, restoring the human dignity of the person in difficulty and/ or pain, of the client.

Going forward, referring to the specific resources  of humanistic social work, after humane personality, we arrive at the expression *humane relationships*, whereby we can to highlight and to delimit the essence, the specificity of the theory, methodology and practice of humanistic social work as the third way in contemporary social work.

If traditional social work, as we seen, is focused, quite strict, on the person in need  and/ or suffering, and critical/ radical social work on the social structure and system, humanistic social work locates somewhere in the middle, her "place" being, so, the human relationships, especially the *humane* relationships, promoting, so, the solidarity, commitment, compathy, humanity, shared well-being and happiness.

For this purpose the work of the professionals and services focuses on exploiting the resources from the micro-community level: families, organizations, neighborhoods, couples, institutions; putting in the background, without disregard, the resources from the macro-level, or the concerns for biological survival and strictly body care.

From this position humanistic social work recognizes and promotes the importance of the resources and defining values of  critical/ radical social work and traditional social work, the community/ society and the human body, but prioritize the importance of the personality/ soul and of the humane relationships, both as resources also as values and goals of the practice, thus tending to complete the complex area of the socio-human existence, structured on the three levels: individual, environmental and societal.

This is also the reason why humanistic social work puts a great emphasis on the humane, psychological-spiritual qualities of professional, core topic of this book.

Operating into the sphere of *human* relationships, the main purpose of its activity is that to transform them in *humane* relationships. The personality and its humane behavior, the psychological-spiritual qualities represents, for this purpose, the means, the essential professional resource that can facilitate the change, through which can humanize the troubled social relationships, the dehumanized, dysfunctional micro-community, the moral, psychological damaged people, in difficulty, suffering, conflict, underdevelopment.

In this way reaching so to perform the specific mission, to determine changes not at the society level, such as critical/ radical social work, where it is the mission of the politician, nor at the body level, where it is the mission of the healthcare professional, but at the human, socio-human level, at the human relationships level, where it is its mission.

In this mission the humanistic practitioner make an "insertion", an involvement. with whole its self, soul, intellect and experience, in the complex assembly of relationships, connections, conflicts, attachments, inter-empathies, compathies, feelings, passions, loves, projects, dramas of the group with problems, detect the dysfunctions, problems, underdevelopments, anomalies, building the diagnostic panel by an etiology and phenomenology of existential-humanistic type, focusing, therefore, on *highlighting the dysfunctions from the human relations level,* the intervention aiming, as has been outlined above, to convert them, by means of his knowledge, experiences, humane personality, soul, and psychological-spiritual qualities, in **humane** *relationships.*

The change for better from the human relationships level, transformed in humane relationships, will generate improvements, impressive qualitative changes at the micro-community level as a whole, as well at the level of each person; the transformative process evolving in cascade, involving humanizing sub-processes at all levels, eliminating many dysfunctions, disorders, problems, sufferings; the new created environment being defined by qualifiers such as spiritual and humane welfare, efficiency, socio-humane cohesion, harmony, solidarity, mutual aid, compathy, responsibility, care, cooperation, humanity, etc.

This environment will impose, ultimately, as a curative solution for many problems and difficult situations, and only to the extent that the professionals and social services manage to lead, generate it, with their activities, measures, conducts can sustain that they operates thoroughly and efficiently, and meet their specific mission, at least in the perspective of the humanistic social work theory and axiology.

Combining thus, in its own and creative way, the resources from the person level, respectively of the humane personality, with the resources from the community level, respectively of the humane relationships, humane community, taking thus elements both from traditional social work and critical/ radical social work, humanistic social work justify their attribute as the third way in theory and practice, with the perspective of imposing, even as dominant, in the contemporary, even upcoming, social work.

In this respect it is presumable that the importance of the humane and spiritual qualities of the professional to increase, the results following to highlights, especially in enhancing the activity effectiveness and achieving the objectives, where the role of these resources and qualities of the professional to imposes almost decisive.

The researches and clinical evidences indicates that, in social work, as well as in other areas of social practices and interventions, psychotherapy, education, etc., empathy is an innate human capability, resource of the practitioners and clients that can be used to increase the efficiency in both the psychological-eudaimonical and the integrative, prosocial objectives.

In humanistic social work the efficiency is high especially when it is considered the direct assistential/ therapeutic relationship between the professional and the client. So, the professional, with the empathetic/ compathetic capacity of his personality and behavior succeeds to have a greater efficiency, both in the objectives involving the welfare and happiness of the client, as well as in those pursuing his empowerment, autonomization, socio-human integration.

Through the empathetic qualities/ skills and resources of the personality, namely the ability to feel the enjoyment (desire, suffering) of the client, the ability to think and experience what the client thinks and feels, the ability to really put in the client's place, to see the world as he/ she see it, the personal provision/ motivation to the other, sympathetic projection of the self, emotional-affective fusion, sympathetic intuition, identification with the client, transfer, etc. the practitioner, in humanistic social work practice, acquires access to the customer's personality/ psychological experience, and, also, acquires an effective method/ way of psychological and social change/ rehabilitation/ empowerment.

So, without any doubt, the level of development of the empathetic capacity/ qualities of the professional, in any philosophy or theoretical orientation, form, doctrine of social work/ welfare, represents essential predictors of effectiveness and fulfillment of the objectives, the more in humanistic social work, where this quality/ resource of the professional exceeds the original psychosocial meaning, instituting so as a core value of the efficiency in practice.

The reason is that, in humanistic social work practice, in caring, therapy, education, etc., by means of the empathetic resources of their own personality, the professional can engage most effective the resources for spiritual, eudaimonical and social rehabilitation of the customer's personality. Spiritual, eudaimonical and social rehabilitation being core objectives and efficiency indicators of this important path of social work at the beginning of the third millennium.

Regarding the importance of spirituality and virtue, as qualities of the professional's personality in activity effectiveness and achieving the objectives, this is given by the fact that the relationship with the client is not objectual but "spiritual", and very complex, and therefore the dominant resources involved must be of this nature.

It is, so, impossible to imagine professional efficiency, in the jobs that involve working with people in need and suffering, without spirituality, virtue, culture, with the soulful welfare and happiness state that it determines. The professionalism, in working with people, being so strongly conditioned by the level of general personal and human development, including the degree of spirituality and charisma/ virtue of the person who provide social services.

At the professionals with developed humane personality the spiritual sensibility and virtue will be imposed as main factors of organization and holistic adjustment of the humanistic professional behavior, becoming a crucial attribute/ source of prosocial action and effective professional practice; without virtue and spirituality the professional being under the dominion of selfishness, impulsiveness, personal undeveloped, laziness, lack of involvement, inactivity, inefficient professional behavior, dominating the defensive behaviors and non-involvement.

That is one of the reasons why the professional's virtue and spirituality becomes, in humanistic social work practice, important sources of efficiency and achievement of the assumed humanistic objectives, of psychological and social change, rehabilitation and empowerment of the people in need or suffering, of the clients.

It is, so, also here, impossible to imagine professional efficiency, in social work practice, and, more so, in humanistic social work practice, practically in all jobs that involve working with people in need and suffering, especially in the activities that involve children, elderly and persons with disabilities, in casework, in caring, education, and therapy, without qualities of the professional such spirituality, virtue, culture, and also without qualities of the professional such happiness and eudemonic-altruistic energy/ motivation.

The studies concludes that the professionalism in working with people is strongly conditioned by the degree of happiness, enthusiam, energy, optimism and personal charisma of the worker. The professional efficiency being correlated with the positive attitudes, with the degree of internal relaxation, the irony and personal happiness.

Not least, personal development, humane development and humanity, practically all the qualities enumerated above, are required, even crucial, in humanistic social work practice, regarding the activity effectiveness and achieving the humanistic objectives, because the practitioner not only provide simple compensatory aid, does not work only for the customers' survive, but seeks to relieve the client suffering, and change his psychological and social condition through his *humane* presence, through its personality's altruism, charisma, virtue and optimism, through its opened mind and soul, through its humanity.

Are crucial, in this sense, their own humane behaviors that need to excel through empathetic, solidarist, altruistic dimension, through agreeableness and charisma. From this point of view, the humanistic practitioner is a model and source for the personality and behavior development of the customers. In this sense, the practitioner's personality, in humanistic social work, must be described through higher, superior humanistic qualifications of composition, structure and development.

The professional's humane sphere and dimension must have a high levels of development and dominant weight in the overall personality structure and composition, in the context of a very high moral and professional conscience, of a humanistic strong structured character, prosocial oriented. In this sense the activity effectiveness and the achievement of the humanistic objectives of practice are directly propor-tional with the weight of the humane sphere and dimension in the overall personality structure and composition, with the presence of some professional's qualities such as morality, virtue, sociality, spiri-tuality, personal development, adaptability, empathy, altruism, gene-rosity, kindness, etc.; in some crucial words: personal development, humane development and humanity.

In activities such as strategy, management, supervision the professio-nal's effectiveness are crucial conditioned of this personal qualities and behaviors, who must to excel, so, through humane, empathetic, solidarist, altruistic dimension, through agreeableness and charisma. From this point of view, the humanistic manager or supervisor is a model and source of education and humane development of the staff, his professional humane personality and behavior being key-factor and source for the worker's personality and behavior development, for all the employees from the professional collectivity.

The strategist, manager, supervisor, educator, in humanistic social work system, is also a humanist intellectual with vast and profound anthropological, philosophical, psychological, pedagogical, sociological, theological knowledge, the values and methods that it promotes relying on a good knowledge of the human, social phenomena, of the man in general also as a person, as individual, of the human rights culture.

Aiming to maximizing the activity effectiveness, the humanistic mana-ger or supervisor, as model and sources, with his humanity, for other professionals, must to work, with his all knowledge, experience, soul and personality, at the formation and development of the professional and humane personality of the worker, of his professional attitudes and behavior, expressed in qualities of personality and conduct as conscientiousness, accountability, empathy/ compathy, agreeableness, happiness, personal/ human development, altruism, optimism, tole-rance, etc.

The aspect highlighting the crucial role of the education/ training in forming and developing the humane and spiritual qualities of the pro-fessional in humanistic, which explain the activity efficiency not only by the qualities of the soul, but also by qualities of the intellect, acquired through culture and education, whether it is about social worker, caregiver, psychologist, educator, manager or supervisor.

In this sense, the humanistic social worker can be described, priority, as a humanist intellectual with vast and profound anthropological, philosophical, psychological, pedagogical, sociological, theological knowledge, the values and methods that he promotes relying on a good knowledge of the human, social phenomena. So, with his qualities, knowledge, experience, soul, personality and behavior, the social worker operates for the formation and development of the client's humane and prosocial personality, for formation and develop-ment of his optimistic and prosocial attitudes, expressed in conducts and qualities of personality as adaptability, conscientiousness, acco-untability, balance, diligence, happiness, virtue – qualities of the pe-rsonality and conduct that would facilitates the personal and social rehabilitation of the client in humanistic social work "system".

Regarding the behavior, activity and objectives of the psychologist, its eficiency in practice, with his humane and spiritual qualities, in huma-nistic social work practice, such as empathy and compathy, spiritual welfare and virtue, happiness and eudemonic-altruistic energy/ moti-vation, personal development, human/ humane development and hu-manity we must to conclude that these play a crucial role, are so some inexhaustible resources, but mostly a therapeutic mobiles, with which the humanistic psychologist achieves their specific objectives in the multidisciplinary team. In this regard, the psychologist's personality or its spiritual qualities shall be described in terms of complex perso-nality, exceptional spiritual traits, soul, empathy, spiritual welfare and happiness, spiritual/ humane sensitivity, agreeableness, charisma, culture and humane intelligence.

The contribution of the humane and spiritual qualities, such as empathy, spirituality, happiness, is decisive regarding the activity effectiveness and achieving the humanistic objectives of activity per-formed by the caregiver or by others workers which are in direct connection with the clients, especially with the children. Unlike the personal/ humane development and humanity/ humanness that are resources, qualities largely passive, of background of the personality, empathy, spiritual welfare and virtue, happiness and eudaimonic-altruistic energy and motivation are active resources, interpersonal, "substances" of the daily communication and interaction with the beneficiaries, especially in residential institutions, foster families, etc.

Instead, therefore, for the manager, strategist and supervisor engaged especially in leadership, planning, monitoring and mentoring activities, are useful, especially, qualities such as personal development, human development and humanity.

Of course, as previously stated in the paper, whether it is done by a social worker or psychologist, by the caregiver or manager, in family and child social work areas, for older people, for those with disabilities or ill, for homeless or people with various forms of addictions, in assessment, planning, intervention and monitoring, in case management, case work, helping or caring, in communities or institutions, on the ground or at the office, the activity must be performed with much professional discipline and scientific rigor.

In this sense, from the humanistic social work axiology position, the professional are first, and foremost, of course, a person with a great soul, but also with a very rigorous scientific and professional training. Their humanistic professional behavior combining so, in an effective way, the sentiment with the information, the soul with the intellect, the humane personality with the professional experience.

Just so, the professional, with his humanistic knowledge, experiences, and qualities such as empathy and compathy, spiritual welfare and virtue, happiness and eudemonic-altruistic energy/ motivation, personal development, humane development and humanity, may contribute effectively to increase the psychological and spiritual welfare of the client, to increase the chances to get social autonomy, fulfilling, thus, one of the most important tasks of humanistic social work:

*to determine profound and durable changes, of the person/ client and community/ family, through human/ humane and spiritual/ cultural empowerment and development, and not only palliative improvements through circumstantial administrative measures and actions of help, support.*

# REFERENCES
# AND WORKS CONSULTED

Achor, S. (2010), *The Happiness Advantage: The Seven Principles of Positive Psychology That Fuel Success and Performance at Work,* Random House Audio.

Adams, E.M. (1997), *A Society Fit for Human Beings* (S U N Y Series in Constructive Postmodern Thought), State University of New York Press.

Ainsworth, M.D.S., Blehar, M.C., Waters, E., Wall, S. (1978), *Patterns of Attachment: A Psychological Study of the Strange Situation.* Hillsdale, NJ: Lawrence Erlbaum Associates.

Allan, J., Pease, B, Briskman L. (2003), *Critical social work,* Melbourne: Allen & Unwin.

Allport, G.W. (1961), *Pattern and growth in personality,* New York: Holt, Rinehart &. Winston.

American Humane Association (2004), *Helping in Child Protective Services: A Competency-Based Casework Handboo*k, Oxford University Press.

Anderson, J., Wiggins Carter, R. (2004), *Diversity perspectives for social work practice.* Boston: Allyn and Bacon.

Antony, M. (2008), *Shyness and Social Anxiety Workbook: Proven, Step-by-Step Techniques for Overcoming your Fear Pape,* Second Edition, New Harbinger Publications.

Aristotle, Robinson, D.N. (1999), *Aristotle's Psychology,* POLOS Ltd.

Arnet, J.J. (2011), *Human Development: A Cultural Approach,* Pearson.

Arts, W., Muffels, R., Meulen, R. (2001), *Solidarity in Health and Social Care in Europe* (Philosophy and Medicine), Kluwer Academic Publisher.

Austin, M.J. (2013), *Social Justice and Social Work: Rediscovering a Core Value of the Profession,* SAGE Publications, Inc.

Bailey, R., Brake, M. (1975). *Radical Social Work,* Pantheon Books.

Balswick, J.O., Balswick, J.K. (2009), *Familia - o perspectivă creştină asupra căminului contemporan,* Editura Casa Cărţii.

Barlow, D.H. (2007), *Clinical Handbook of Psychological Disorders*, Fourth Edition: A Step-by-Step Treatment Manual (Barlow: Clinical Handbook of Psychological Disorders), The Guilford Press.

Bandura, A. (1975), *Social Learning & Personality Development*, NY: Holt, Rinehart & Winston, INC.

Bandura, A., Locke, A. E. (2003), Negative self-efficacy and goal effects revisited. *Journal of Applied Psychology.*

Barker, R. L. (2003), *The social work dictionary* (5th ed.), Washington, DC: NASW Press.

Barty, J., Redding, E. (2013), *Reforming Social Work: Improving Social Worker Recruitment, Training and Retention*, Policy Exchange.

Batson, C.D. (2011), *Altruism in Humans*. New York: Oxford University Press.

Baumeister, B.R.F., Bushman, B.J. (2013), *Social Psychology and Human Nature*, Cengage Learning.

Byers, S.C. (2012), *Perception, Sensibility, and Moral Motivation in Augustine: A Stoic-Platonic Synthesis*, Cambridge University Press.

Bean, J.S. (2013), *Finding Real Love through God's Word (Relationship Guide for Women Seeking Soulmates),* Kindle Edition, Amazon Digital Services, Inc.

Beaulieu, E. (2012), *A Guide for Nursing Home Social Workers*, Second Edition, Springer Publishing Company.

Beaumont, H., Cobb Jr., J.B. (2012), *Toward a Spiritual Psychotherapy: Soul as a Dimension of Experience*, North Atlantic Books.

Beck, U. (1992), *Risk Society - Towards a New Modernity,* London: Sage.

Benner , D.G. (2011), *Soulful Spirituality: Becoming Fully Alive and Deeply Human*, Brazos Press (March.

Bellinger A, Elliott T. (2011), *What are you looking at? The potential of appreciative inquiry as a research approach for social work*. British Journal of Social Work 41: 708–725.

Berger, P.L., Luckmann, T. (1967), *The Social Construction of Reality: A Treatise in the Sociology of Knowledge,* Anchor.

Bergin, A.E. (2003), *Casebook for a Spiritual Strategy in Counseling and Psychotherapy*, Amer Psychological Assn.

Bergson, H. (2007), *Mind-Energy ,*Palgrave Macmillan

Berkowitz, N. (1996), *Humanistic Approaches to Health Care: Focus on Social Work (Social Work in a Changing World)*, Venture Press.

Biestek, F.P, Gehrig, C.C. (1978), *Client Self-Determination in Social Work*, Loyola Press.

Boudon., R. (1971), *La crise de la sociologie*, Geneve: Droz.

Bounds, M. (2010), *Welfare Policy: Feminist Critiques*, Wipf & Stock Pub.

Bowling, D., Ho attachments ffman, D. (2003), *Bringing Peace Into the Room: How the Personal Qualities of the Mediator Impact the Process of Conflict Resolution*, Jossey-Bass.

Bowlby J. (1999), *Attachment. Attachment and Loss* (vol. 1) (2nd ed.), New York: Basic Books.R. Brown.

Bradford, D.L., Burke, W.W. (2005), *Organization Development*, San Francisco: Pfeiffer.

Briar, S., Miller, H. (1971), *Problems and Issues in Social Casework*, New York: Columbia University Press.

Buechler, S.M. (2008), *Critical Sociology,* Paradigm Publishers.

Bywater, I. (2010), *Aristotelis Ethica Nicomachea* (Cambridge Library Collection - Classics) (Ancient Greek Edition), Cambridge University Press.

Canda, E.R., Furman, L.D. (2009), *Spiritual Diversity in Social Work Practice: The Heart of Helping,* Oxford University Press.

Chansky, T.E. (2008), *Freeing Your Child from Negative Thinking: Powerful, Practical Strategies to Build a Lifetime of Resilience, Flexibility, and Happiness,* Da Capo Lifelong Books.

Chelf, C.P. (1992), *Controversial Issues in Social Welfare Policy: Government and the Pursuit of Happiness (Controversial Issues in Public Policy),* SAGE Publications, Inc.

Cicchetti, D., Carlson, V. (1989), *Child Maltreatment: Theory and Research on the Causes and Consequences of Child Abuse and Neglect,* Cambridge University Press.

Cloke C., Davies M. (1995), *Participation and empowerment in Chid Protection,* London, Pitman.

Cojocaru, S. (2013), *Appreciative Inquiry in Social Work: Theories and practices,* LAP LAMBERT Academic Publishing.

Coleman, C. (1998), *The Volunteer,* Grand Central Publishing.

Collins, D., Jordan, C., Coleman, H. (2010), *An Introduction to Family Social Work,* Belmont, Brooks/Cole.

Comte, A. (2004), *Catéchisme positiviste ou Sommaire exposition de la religion universelle,* Kindle Edition, EbooksLib.

Corey, G. (2012), *Theory and Practice of Counseling and Psychotherapy*, Cengage Learning.

Cottraux, J. (2003), *Terapiile cognitive*, Iași: Editura Polirom.

Cosman, D. (2010), *Psihologie medicală*, Iași: Editura Polirom.

Cournoyer, B.R. (2013), *The Social Work Skills Workbook,* 7 edition, Cengage Learning.

Gilligan, P. and Furness, S. (2006), *The Role of Religion and Spirituality in Social Work Practice: views and experiences of social workers and students*, British Journal of Social Work, 36 (4), 617 637.

Cross, M.C. (2001), *Becoming a Therapist: A Manual for Personal and Professional Development,* Routledge.

Cuin, C.H. (2006), The nomologic approach in sociology, *Revue suisse de sociologie*, Switzerland, Seismo Verlag.

Cummins, K., Sevel, J.A., Pedrick, L. (2011), *Social Work Skills for Beginning Direct Practice: Text, Workbook, and Interactive Web Based Case Studies,* (3rd Edition), Pearson.

Cusick, A. (2011), *The Psychology of the Soul*, CreateSpace, Charleston SC, an Amazon.com Company.

Danesh, H.B. (1994), *Psychology of Spirituality*, Paradigm Publishing.

DeVries, R., Zan, B. (2012), *Moral Classrooms, Moral Children: Creating a Constructivist Atmosphere in Early Education,* Teachers College Press.

Doherty, W.J. (1996), *Soul Searching: Why Psychotherapy Must Promote Moral Responsibility,* Basic Books.

Doise, W., Deschamp, J.C., Mugny, G. (1996), *Psihologie socială experimentală*, Editura Polirom.

Dominelli, L., Mc Leod, E. (1989), *Feminist Social Work*, MacMillian Press Ltd.

Dominelli, L. (2002), *Anti-Oppressive Social Work Theory and Practice*, Palgrave Macmillan.

Durkheim, E. (2004), *Sociologia - regulile metodei sociologice*, Editura Antet.

Edwin, L. (2007), *Projective Psychology - Clinical Approaches To The Total Personality*, Pratt Press.

Elkin, D. (2009), *Humanistic Psychology: A Clinical Manifesto. A Critique of Clinical Psychology and the Need for Progressive Alternatives*, Universities of the Rockies Press.

Elrefai, T. (2013), *Diversity to Unity: A journey to a vision of humanism*, Commoners.

Ellis, A. (1974), *Humanistic Psychotherapy: The Rational-Emotive Approach*, Mcgraw-Hill.

Ellenhorn, R. (1988), *Toward a Humanistic Social Work: Social Work for Conviviality,* New Jersey: Association for Humanist Sociology.

Ellis A., Abrams, M., Abrams, L.D. (2008), *Personality Theories: Critical Perspectives,* SAGE Publications, Inc.

Else, J.F. (1977), *Purposive social change: A radical humanist perspective,* Social Work Foundation, School of Social Work, University of Iowa.

Elson, M. (1988), *Self Psychology in Clinical Social Work*, W. W. Norton & Company.

Endler, N., Parker, J. (1992), Interactionism revisited: Reflections on the continuing crisis in the personality area, în *European Journal of Personality*, 6, pp. 177-198, http://www.ourfutureenvironment.org/personality/wp-content/uploads/2010/08/endler_ interactionism.pdf.

Erikson, E. H., Erikson, J.M. (1998), *The Life Cycle Completed*, W W Norton & Co Inc.

Feldman, R. (1985), Reliability and Justification, în *The Monist*, Buffalo, NY: Open Court Publishing Company.

Ferréol, G. (1998), *Dicţionar de sociologie*, Iaşi: Editura Polirom

Filip, J., McDaniel, N., Schene, P. (1999), *Helping in child protective services. A competency-based case-work handbook*, American Human Asociation, Englewood, Colorado.

Fox, P.J. (2011), *Heart of a Caregiver: Touching Lives with Compassion and Care*, Simple Truths.

Frankl, V. (2009), *Teoria şi terapia nevrozelor. Introducere în logoterapie şi analiza existenţială*, trad. în lb. română de Daniela Ştefănescu, Bucureşti: Editura Trei.

Freud, S., Strachey, J., Hitchens, C., Gay, P. (2010), *Civilization and Its Discontents* (Complete Psychological Works of Sigmund Freud), W. W. Norton & Company.

Friedman, H.S., Schustack, M.W. (2010), *Personality: Classic Theories and Modern Research* (5th Edition), Pearson.

Garfinkel, H. (2006), *Seeing sociologically*, Boulder, CO, Paradigm Publishers.

Game, A. (1991), *Undoing the Social: Towards a Deconstructive Sociology*, Toronto, University of Toronto Press.

Gammer, C. (2008), *The Child's Voice in Family Therapy: A Systemic Perspective*, W. W. Norton & Company.

Garrigou-Lagrange, R., Cummins, P. (1950), *Reality—A Synthesis Of Thomistic Thought*, St. Louis, Mo.: Herder.

Gerdes, K. E. Segal, E. A. (2009), A social work model of empathy. Advances in Social Work Practice, *Social Work* 10(2), 114-127.

Gerdes, K. E., Segal, E. A. (2011), The importance of empathy for social work practice: Integrating new science, *Social Work*, 56(2), 141-148.

Gerdes, K. E. (2011), Introduction: 21st century conceptualizations of empathy: Implications for social work practice and research, *Journal of Social Service Research*, 37(3), 226-229.

Gilgun, J.F. (2008), *The Four Cornerstones of Evidence-Based Practice in Social Work*, Jane Gilgun Books.

Gill, D.W. (2000), *Becoming Good: Building Moral Character*, IVP Books.

Gill, M. (2011), Educating the Professional Social Worker: Challenges and Prospects, în *Revista de asistență socială*, nr. 4, pp. 30-41, Iași: Editura Polirom.

Ginsberg, L.H., Ginsberg, L. (2008), *Management and Leadership in Social Work Practice and Education,* Council on Social Work Education.

Goldstein, H. (1984), *Creative Change: A Cognitive-Humanistic Approach to Social Work Practice*, Routledge.

Goldstein, E.G. (1995), *Ego Psychology and Social Work Practice*: 2nd Edition, The Free Press.

Gonzalez-Mena, J. (2012), *Child, Family, and Community: Family-Centered Early Care and Education,* Pearson.

Goroff, N. (1981), Humanism and Social Work Paradoxes, Problems, and Promises, *The Journal of Sociology & Social Welfare*: Vol. 8: Iss. 1.

Grinnell Jr, R.M., Unrau, Y.A., (2010), *Social Work Research and Evaluation: Foundations of Evidence-Based Practice*, Oxford University Press.

Haidt, J. (2008), *Teoria fericirii,* București: Editura Almatea.

Hall, E. (1966), *The Hidden Dimension*, New York, Anchor Books.

Harel, I., Papert, S. (1991), *Constructionism,* Norwood, Ablex Publishing Corporation.

Hamblin, R. L., Buckholdt, D., Ferritor, D., Kozloff, M., Blackwell, L. (1971), *The Humanization Processes: A Social, Behavioral Analysis of Children's Problems*, Krieger Pub Co.

Hardcastle, A. ( 2011), *Theories and Skills for Social Workers,* 3 edition, Oxford University Press.

Harkness, D. (2002), *Supervision in Social Work,* Columbia University Press.

Healy, L. (2008), *International social work: Professional action in an interdependent world.* 2d ed. Oxford: Oxford Univ. Press.

Heidegger, M. (1995), *Introducere in metafizică,* București: Editura Humanitas

Heidegger, M. (1995), *Timp și Ființă,* București: Editura Jurnalul Literar.

Habermas J., Lenhardt, C. (2001), *Moral Consciousness and Communicative Action,* The MIT Press.

Hepworth, D. H. și al. (2009), *Direct Social Work Practice: Theory and Skills,* 8 edition Cengage Learning.

Hobson, J.A. (1933), *Rationalism and Humanism*, London: Watts & Co.

Hoffman, M.L. (2000), *Empathy and moral development: Implications for caring and justice.* New York: Cambridge University Press.

Horner, N., Kindred, M. (1997), *Using Humanist/Existential Theories in Social Work (Using Theories in Social Work)*, Open Learning Foundation.

Howe, D. (1995), *Attachment Theory for Social Work Practice*, Palgrave Macmillan.

Howe, D. (2009), *A Brief Introduction to Social Work Theory,* Palgrave Macmillan.

Hughes, D.A. (2000), *Facilitating Developmental Attachment: The Road to Emotional Recovery and Behavioral Change in Foster and Adopted Children,* Jason Aronson, Inc.

Humanistische Akademie. (1998). *Humanistische Sozialarbeit*, Berlin: Humanistische Akademie. Series: Humanismus aktuell, H. 3. Jg. 2.

Ife, J. (2012), *Human Rights and Social Work: Towards Rights-Based Practice,* Cambridge University Press.

Illomen, K. (2011), *A Social and Economic Theory of Consumption*, Palgrave Macmillan.

Inderbitzin, M.L., Bates, C.A., Gainey, R.R. (2012), *Deviance and Social Control: A Sociological Perspective,* SAGE Publications.

James, W. (1981), *Pragmatism: A New Name for Some Old Ways of Thinking*, Hackett Publishing.

Jex, S.M., Gudanowski D.M. (1992), Efficacy beliefs and work stress: An exploratory study. *Journal of Organizational Behavior* .

Jones, C. (1993), *New Perspectives on the Welfare State in Europe,* London: Routledge.

Jones , D. (2014), *Using a Humanistic Solution Focused Approach with Parents and Families to Reduce Anti-Social Behaviour and Youth Offending: An Evidence-Based Approach for Professionals in Social Work Practice,* Lulu.com.

Jung, C.G. (1981), *The Archetypes and The Collective Unconscious* (Collected Works of C.G. Jung Vol.9 Part 1), Princeton University Press.

Jung, C.G. (1994), *Puterea sufletului*. Antologie, Bucureşti: Editura Anima.

Kadushin, A., Harkness, D. (2014), *Supervision in Social Work*, 5e, Columbia University Press.

Kant, I. (1998), *Critica raţiunii pure*, Bucureşti: Editura I R I.

Kant, I. (2005), *Prolegomene*, Piteşti: Editura Paralela 45.

Kelly G.A. (1991), *The Psychology of Personal Constructs*, London: Routledge.

Kosman, A. (2013), *The Activity of Being: An Essay on Aristotle's Ontology*, Harvard University Press.

Kostelnik, M. (2011), *Guiding Children's Social Development and Learning (What's New in Early Childhood),* Cengage Learning.

Kotarba, J.A., Johnson, J.M. (2002), *Postmodern existential sociology,* Walnut Creek, CA, Alta Mira.

Kreeft, P. (1992), *Back to Virtue: Traditional Moral Wisdom for Modern Moral Confusion*, Ignatius Press.

Krill, D.F. (1978), *Existential social work*, New York: Free Press,

Kramer-Moore, D., Moore, M. (2012), *Destructive Myths in Family Therapy: How to Overcome Barriers to Communication by Seeing and Saying -- A Humanistic Perspective*, Wiley-Blackwell.

Kroeber, A. L., Kluckhohn, C. (1952), *Culture: A Critical Review of Concepts and Definitions*, New York: Vintage Books.

Lacan, J. (1991), *The Seminar of Jacques Lacan: Book II: The Ego in Freud's Theory and in the Technique of Psychoanalysis*, W. W. Norton & Company, 1991.

Langan, T. (2009), *Human Being: A Philosophical Anthropology*, University of Missouri Press.

Lavalette, M. (ed.) (2011), *Radical Social Work Today: Social Work at the Crossroads*, Bristol: Policy Press.

Lerner, M. (2011), *Education And A Radical Humanism: Notes Toward A Theory Of The Educational Crisis,* Licensing, LLC.

Levi-Strauss, C. (1969), *The elementary structures of kinship*, Beacon Press, Boston.

Lietz, C. A. și al. (2011), The empathy assessment index (EAI): A confirmatory factor analysis of a five component model of empathy, *Journal of the Society for Social Work and Research*, 2(2), 104-124.

Lilienthal, D.E. (1967), *Management: A Humanist Art*, Carnegie Institute of Technology.

Lock, A., Strong, T. (2010), *Social constructionism: Sources and stirrings in theory and practice*, New York: Cambridge University Press.

Lukacs, G. (1978), *Ontology of Social Being*, Volume 1, Hegel, Merlin Press.

Madanes, C. (2006), *The Therapist as Humanist, Social Activist, and Systemic Thinker*, Zeig, Tucker & Theisen, Inc.

May, G.G. (1987), *Will and Spirit: A Contemplative Psychology*, HarperOne.

Maslow, A.H. (1993), *The Farther Reaches of Human Nature*, Penguin / Arkana.

Maslow, A.H. (2008), *Motivatie si personalitate*, București: Editura Trei.

Maslow, A.H. (2011), *Toward A Psychology of Being* - Reprint of 1962 Edition, Martino Fine Books.

Masters, A., Wallace, H.R. (2010), *Development for Life and Work,* 10 edition, Cengage Learning.

Maritain, J. 1956), *Existence and the Existent: An Essay on Christian Existentialism*, trans. L. Galantiere and G.B. Phelan, New York: Image.

McBeath, G., & Webb, S. A. (2002). Virtue ethics and social work: Being lucky, realistic, and not doing one's duty. British Journal of Social Work, 32, 1015-1036.

Mc Call, L.A. (2001), *The McCall Body Balance Method : Simple Concepts for Ageless Movement*, Lisa Mccall.

McLaren, N. (2010), *Humanizing Psychiatrists: Toward a Humane Psychiatry,* Future Psychiatry Press.

Mille, S. (2009), *The Moral Foundations of Social Institutions: A Philosophical Study,* Cambridge University Press.

Miller, C. (2013), *Moral Character: An Empirical Theory,* Oxford University Press.

Miller, J.P. (1999), *Education and the Soul: Toward a Spiritual Curriculum,* State University of New York Press.

Miller, J.P. (2005), *Holistic Learning And Spirituality In Education: Breaking New Ground,* State University of New York Press.

Minsky, M. (2007), *The Emotion Machine: Commonsense Thinking, Artificial Intelligence and the Future of the Human Mind,* Simon & Schuster.

Mjoset, L. (2009), The contextualist approch to social science metodology, în David, B., Ragin, C.C. (coord), *The SAGE hanbook of case-based metods,* London: SAGE Publication Ltd., pp. 39-68.

Moody R., Carroll, D. (1997), *The Five Stages of the Soul: Charting the Spiritual Passages That Shape Our Lives,* New York: Anchor Books.

Moghaddam, F.M. (1998), *Social psychology,* New York: W.H. Freeman end Company.

Moore, T. (1994), *Care of the Soul : A Guide for Cultivating Depth and Sacredness in Everyday Life,* HarperPerennial.

Moore, T. (1994), *Soul Mates: Honoring the Mystery of Love and Relationship,* HarperPerennial.

Moustakas, C. (1966), *Existential Child Therapy,* Basic Books Inc.

Moustakas, C. (1994), *Phenomenological Research Methods,* Thousand Oaks, California: Sage Publications.

Mowrer, E.R. (1972), *Family Disorganization: An Introduction to a Sociological Analysis,* Arno Press and The New York Times.

Mullaly, B. (2006), *The New Structural Social Work: Ideology, Theory, Practice,* 3rd (third) Edition, Oxford University Press.

Mullaly, B. (2002), *Challenging Oppression: A Critical Social Work Approach,* Oxford University Press.

Muntean, A. (2013), *Adopţia şi ataşamentul copiilor separaţi de părinţii biologici,* Iaşi: Editura Polirom.

Myers, D. G. (2004, *Theories of Emotion. Psychology,* Worth Publishers, Găsit la adresa: www.scribd.com/doc/39094849/Emotion.

Neamţu, G. (coord) (2011), *Tratat de asistenţă socială,* Ediţia a II –a, Iaşi: Editura Polirom.

Nelson, C.A. (2013), R*omania's Abandoned Children: Deprivation, Brain Development, and the Struggle for Recovery,* Harvard University Press.

Netting, F.E., Kettner, P.M., McMurtry, S.L., Thomas, M.L. (2011), *Social Work Macro Practice* (5th Edition), Pearson.

Nietzsche, F. (1999), *Voința de putere: încercare de transmutare a tuturor valorilor* (fragmente postume), traducere de Claudiu Baciu, Oradea: Editura Aion.

Nietzsche, F. (2013), *Ecce Homo. Cum devii ceea ce esti,* București: Editura Humanitas.

Noam, G.G., Wren, T.E. (1993), *Moral Self: Building a Better Paradigm,* The MIT Press.

Noddings, N. 2003, *Happiness and education,* Cambridge University Press.

Nolan, P., Lenski, G. (2010), *Human Societies: An Introduction to Macrosociology,* Oxford University Press.

O'Hare, T. (2005), *Evidence-Based Practices for Social Workers: An Interdisciplinary Approach,* Lyceum Books.

Osho (2001), *Inteligența, Reacționează creativ la prezent,* București: Pro Editură și Tipografie.

Outhwaite, W. (2006), *The Future of Society* (Blackwell Manifestos), Wiley-Blackwell.

Panter-Brick, C., Smith, M.T. (2000), *Abandoned Children,* Cambridge University Press.

Parris, M. 2013), *An introduction to social work practice,* Open University Press.

Parsons, T. (1978), *Social Systems and the Evolution of Action Theory,* New York: Free Press.

Pavlovich, K., Krahnke, K. (2013), *Organizing through Empathy* (Routledge Studies in Management, Organizations and Society), Routledge.

Payne, M. (2011), *Humanistic Social Work. Core Principles in Practice,* Basingstoke, Hampshire, England: Palgrave Macmillan.

Payne, M. (2005), *Modern Social Work Theory,* Lyceum Books.

*Patterson, C. H. (1973), Humanistic education,* Englewood Prentice.

Pelzer, D. (1997), *The Lost Boy: A Foster Child's Search for the Love of a Family,* Health Communications.

Punalekar, S.P. (1983), *Deprivation, institutionalisation and development: A study of child welfare institutions in Gujarat,* Centre for Social Studies.

Hamilton, E., Cairns, H., Cooper, L. (2005), *The Collected Dialogues of Plato: Including the Letters,* Princeton University Press.

Plotnik, R., Kouyoumdjian, H. (2007), *Introduction to Psychology,* Belmont: Wadsworth Publishing Company.

Pound, R. (1996), *Social Control through Law*, Transaction Publishers.

Reamer, F. G. (1993), *The philosophical foundations of social work*, New York: Columbia University.

Rickert, H. (1986), *The Limits of Concept Formation in Natural Science,* Cambridge University Press.

Rifkin, J. (2009), The *Empathic Civilization: The Race to Global Consciousness in a World in Crisis,* Tarcher.

Robbins, A. (2001), *Putere nemărginită*, Bucureşti: Editura Amaltea

Robert, L., Mathis, R.L., Nica, P.C., Rusu, C. (1998), *Managementul resurselor umane,* Bucureşti: Editura. Economică.

Roberts, A.R., Yeager, KR. (2006), *Foundations of Evidence-Based Social Work Practice*, Oxford University Press.

Rocco, M. (1997), Religie şi creaţie, în M. Zlate (coord), *Psihologia vieţii cotidiene,* Editura Polirom.

Rogers, C. R. (1951), *Client-Centered Therapy: Its Current Practice, Implications, and Theory*, Boston: Houghton Mifflin.

Rogers, C.R. (1959), A Theory of Therapy, Personality and Interpersonal Relationships as Developed in the Client-centered Framework. In (ed.) S. Koch, *Psychology: A Study of a Science,* New York: McGraw Hill.

Rogers, C.R. (1977), *On Personal Power: Inner Strength and Its Revolutionary Impact*, Delacorte Press.

Rogers, C.R. (1980), *A Way of Being*, Boston: Houghton Mifflin

Rogers, C.R. ( 2008), *A deveni o persoana*, Bucureşti, Editura: Trei.

Ross, E.A. (2002), *Social Control: A Survey of the Foundations of Order,* University Press of the Pacific.

Rubin, A, Babbi, E.R. (2012), *Research Methods for Social Work,* Brooks/Cole Empowerment.

Rudman, J. (2013), *Supervisor,* National Learning Corporation.

Rutter, S.M, Smith, D.J. (1995), *Psychosocial Disorders in Young People: Time Trends and Their Causes*, Wiley.

Sandu, A. (2013*), Social Work Practice: Research Techniques and Intervention Models: From Problem Solving to Appreciative Inquiry*, LAP LAMBERT Academic Publishing.

Saran, P. (1998), *Tantra: Hedonism in Indian Culture*, DK Printworld.

Sartre, J.P. (2004), *Fiinţa si neantul. Eseu de ontologie fenomenologică*, Editura Paralela 45, Bucureşti.

Sarvarovschi, O.A. (2009), Climatul familial și definițiile valorice elaborate de minorul delincvent în actul infracțional, în *Revista de Asistență Socială*, Nr. 3-4, Editura Polirom, pp. 153-162.

Schooler, J.E. (2010), *Wounded Children, Healing Homes: How Traumatized Children Impact Adoptive and Foster Families,* NavPress.

Schreurs, A. (2001), *Psychotherapy and Spirituality: Integrating the Spiritual Dimension into Therapeutic Practice,* Jessica Kingsley Pub.

Segal, E.A., Gerdes, K.E., Steiner, S. (2010), *An introduction to the profession of social work* (3rd ed.), Belmont, CA: Brooks/Cole.

Seidman, B.F. (2004), *Toward A New Political Humanism,* Prometheus Books.

Seligman, M.E., Csikszentmihalzi, P. (2000), Positive Pshyhology, în *American Psychologist,* vol. LV, nr. 1.

Seligman, M. E. P. (2002), *Authentic Happiness.* New York: Free Press.

Schutz A. (1972), *The Phenomenology of the Social World,* London: Heinemann Educational Books.

Shebib, B. (2002), *Choices: Counseling Skills for Social Workers and Other Professionals,* Pearson.

Shemmings, D. (2011), *Understanding Disorganized Attachment: Theory and Practice for Working With Children and Adults,* Jessica Kingsley.

Sinnott-Armstrong, W. (2014), *Moral Psychology: Free Will and Moral Responsibility.* A Bradford Book.

Smith, D. (2004), *Social work and evidence based practice,* London: Jessica, Kingsley.

Sousa, D.A. (2010), *Mind, Brain and Education: Neuroscience Implications for the Classroom,* Hardcover Solution Tree.

Stairs, J. (2000), *Listening for the Soul: Pastoral Care and Spiritual Direction,* Fortress Press.

Stangor, C. (2004), *Social groups in action and interaction,* New York: Psychology Press.

Steiner, R. (1996), *The education of the child, and early lectures on education,* Hudson, N.Y.: Anthroposophic Press.

Stern, E.M., Kramer, S.Z. (1995), *Transforming the Inner and Outer Family: Humanistic and Spiritual Approaches to Mind-Body Systems Therapy,* Routledge.

Stone, J.D. (1999), Soul Psychology: How to Clear Negative Emotions and Spiritualize Your Life, Wellspring/Ballantine.

Storr, A. (1992), *The Integrity of the Personality,* Ballantine Books.

Stefaroi, P. (2007), Specificul managementului (eficient) în domeniul asistenței sociale, în *Revista de Asistență Socială,* nr. 3, Iași: Editura Polirom.

Stefaroi, P. (2008), Tulburări de dezvoltare socio-afectivă ale copilului instituţionalizat, în *Revista de Asistenţă Socială*, Nr. 1-2, Iaşi: Editura Polirom.

Stefaroi, P. (2009), Perspectiva umanistă asupra clientului în asistenţa sociala, în *Revista de Asistenţă Socială*, Nr. 1-2, Iaşi: Editura Polirom.

Stefaroi, P. (2009), *Teoria fericirii în asistenţa socială. De la managementul îngrijirii la managementul fericirii*, Iaşi: Editura Lumen.

Stefaroi, P. (2012), Paradigma umanistă a asistenţei sociale sau scurtă introducere în asistenţa socială umanistă, in *Revista de Asistenţă Socială*, Nr. 1, Iaşi: Editura Polirom.

Stefaroi, P. (2013), *Calitati psihologic-sufletesti ale profesionistului in asistenta sociala umanista*, CreateSpace, Charleston SC, an Amazon.com Company.

Stefaroi, P. (2014), *Calitati psihologic-sufletesti ale profesionistului in asistenta sociala umanista – The HUMANISTIC SOCIAL WORK Project: Humanistic Social Work – The Third Way in Theory and Practice*, CreateSpace, Charleston SC, an Amazon.com Company.

Stets, J. E., Carter, M. J. (2011), The moral self: Applying identity theory. *Social Psychology Quarterly*, 74, 192–215.

Tanzi, E.R., Chopra, D. (2013), *Super Brain: Unleashing the Explosive Power of Your Mind to Maximize Health, Happiness, and Spiritual Well-Being*, Harmony.

Tiryakian, E.A. (1962), *Sociologism and existentialism, two perspectives on the individual and society*, Englewood Cliffs, N.J., Prentice-Hall.

Thomas, S.C. (1996), *A sociological perspective on contextualism*, în *Journal of Counseling and Development*, JCD, July 1, 74(6), 529-541, http://www.highbeam.com/doc/1P3-10006742.html.

Timberlake, E.M., Cutler, M.M. (2000), *Developmental Play Therapy in Clinical Social Work*, Pearson.

Tsui, M. (2004), *Social Work Supervision: Contexts and Concepts*, SAGE Publications.

Vincent, J-D., Hughes, J. (1990), *The Biology of Emotions*, Blackwell Pub.

Walsh, M. (2006), *Nurse Practitioners: Clinical Skill and Professional Issues*, 2 edition, Butterworth-Heinemann.

Ward, C.C. (2010), *Strength-Centered Counseling: Integrating Postmodern Approaches and Skills With Practice*, SAGE Publications, Inc.

Watson, D., Clark, L. A., Tellegen, A. (1988), Development and validation of brief measures of positive affect and negative affect, în *Journal of Personality and Social Psychology*, Washington: American Psychological Association. Găsit la adresa http://www.apa.org/pubs/journals/psp/.

Watt, I. (1957), *The Rise of the Novel*, Berkeley, University of California.

Webb, N.B. (2005), *Working with Traumatized Youth in Child Welfare (Social Work Practice with Children and Families*, The Guilford Press.

Weber, M. (2001), Introducere în sociologia religiilor, Iaşi: Institutul European.

Weissman, D. (2000), *A social ontology*, London: Yale University Press.

Weisman, C. S., Nathanson, C. A. (1985). Professional satisfaction and client outcomes: A comparative organizational analysis. *Medical Care*, 23, 1179–1192.

Wheeler, G. (1991), *Gestalt reconsidered*, New York: Gardner Press.

Whitaker, C. W. A. (2002), *Aristotle's De Interpretatione: Contradiction and Dialectic* (Oxford Aristotle Studies), Oxford University Press.

Williams, B. (1993), *Introducere în etică*, Bucureşti: Editura Alternative.

Wilber, K. (2000), *Integral Psychology: Consciousness, Spirit, Psychology, Therapy*, Shambhala.

William K. F. (2012), *Opening to the Sacred: A Humanist Approach to Holistic Spirituality*, Premium Prose Publishing.

Wing Sue, D. (2006), *Multicultural social work practice*, USA: WILEY.

Wommack, A. (2010), *Spirit, Soul and Body*, Harrison House.

Young, P.T. (1961), *Motivation and Emotion*, John Wiley & Sons Inc.

Zamfir. E. (2008), The new human model proposed by humanist pychology. Types of conflict resolution, in *Social Work Review*, nr. 1-2, pp 3-28.

Zastrow, Ch. (2009), *Introduction to Social Work and Social Welfare: Empowering People,* Thomson Brooks/Cole.

Znaniecki, F. (1969), *On humanistic sociology*, Chicago: University of Chicago Press.

*** www.books.google.ro/.

*** www.copsi.ro/.

*** www.cnasr.ro/.

*** ifsw.org/.

*** www.ohchr.org/EN/UDHR.

*** www.lyceumbooks.com/HumanisticSocialWork.htm.

*** www.scribd.com/.

*** www.socialworkers.org/.

*** www.un.org/en/documents/udhr/.

Petru Stefaroi:
Humane & Spiritual Qualities of the Professional in Humanistic Social Work:
*Humanistic Social Work – The THIRD WAY in Theory and Practice*

*The Version Entirely in English*

December, 2014


Printed by CreateSpace, Charleston SC,
an Amazon.com Company, USA

---

Available on Amazon.com,
CreateSpace.com, and others retail outlets

http://www.amazon.com/
https://www.createspace.com/

CreateSpace
4900 LaCross Road
North Charleston, SC 29406

---

Author's email adress:
petrustefaroi@yahoo.com

The
**HUMANISTIC**
**SOCIAL WORK**
Project

www.ingramcontent.com/pod-product-compliance
Lightning Source LLC
Chambersburg PA
CBHW070640290526
45790CB00001B/149